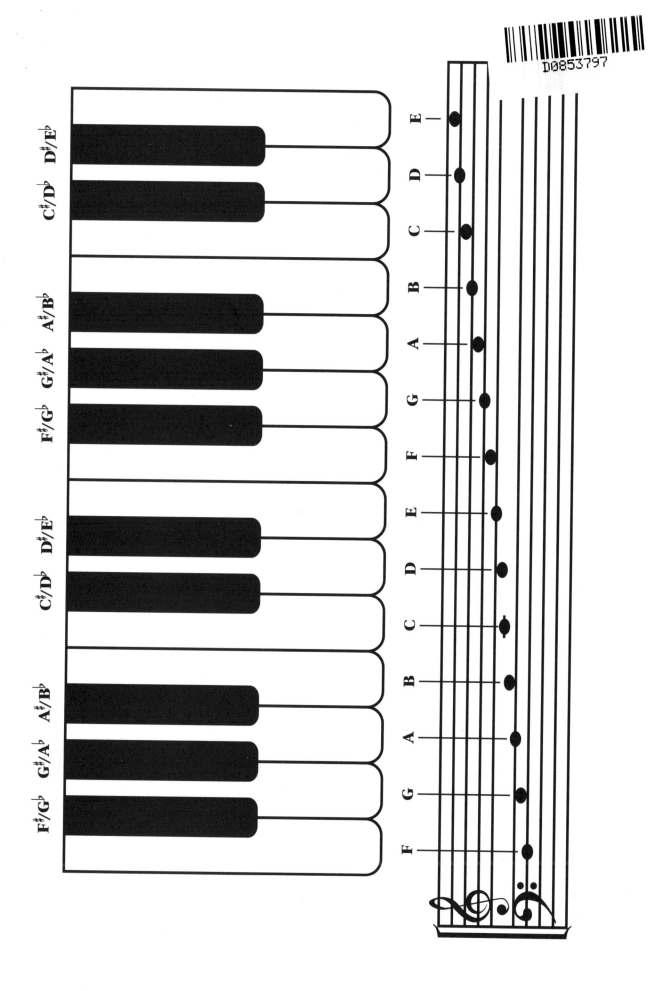

# Silver Burdett
# MAKING MUSIC

## Program Authors

Jane Beethoven
Susan Brumfield
Patricia Shehan Campbell
David N. Connors
Robert A. Duke
Judith A. Jellison

Rita Klinger
Rochelle Mann
Hunter C. March
Nan L. McDonald
Marvelene C. Moore
Mary Palmer
Konnie Saliba

Will Schmid
Carol Scott-Kassner
Mary E. Shamrock
Sandra L. Stauffer
Judith Thomas
Jill Trinka

## Recording Producers

Rick Baitz
Rick Bassett
Joseph Joubert
Bryan Louiselle

Tom Moore
J. Douglas Pummill
Michael Rafter
Buryl Red, EXECUTIVE PRODUCER

Buddy Skipper
Robert Spivak
Jeanine Tesori
Linda Twine

## Scott Foresman

**Editorial Offices:** Parsippany, New Jersey • Glenview, Illinois • New York, New York
**Sales Offices:** Parsippany, New Jersey • Duluth, Georgia • Glenview, Illinois
Coppell, Texas • Ontario, California

ISBN: 0-382-34346-8

# Contents

# Steps to Making Music

# Paths to Making Music

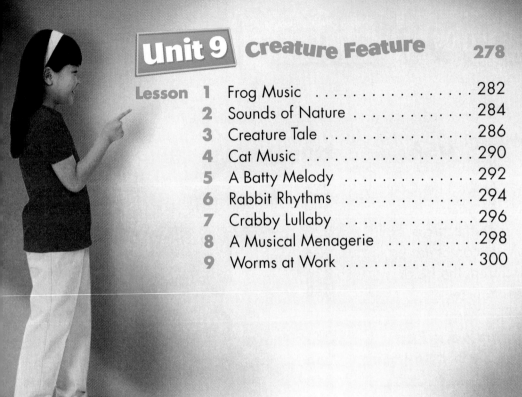

# Unit 9 Creature Feature 278

# Unit 10 Our Planet Earth 304

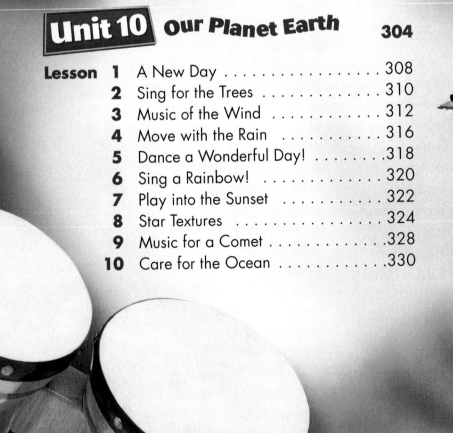

## Unit 11   Perform a Story    332

## Unit 12   Celebrate the Season    358

# STEPS TO MAKING MUSIC

## Let the Good Times Begin!

Anyone can make music. You can sing, move, play, listen to, and create music. Get ready to begin making music!

# Let the Music Begin!

## Songs That Entertain

Bill Shontz wrote this song. Sometimes he works with his partner, Gary Rosen. They call themselves Rosenshontz.

**Move** in cool ways as you **listen** to "Gonna Have a Good Time."

# Gonna Have a Good Time

*Words and Music by Bill Shontz*

1. Lis - ten  to  the sound  of  the  mu - sic,
2. Lis - ten  to  the sound  of  the  mu - sic,

Lis - ten  to  the sound  of  the flute;
Lis - ten  to  the sound  of  the drums;

Lis - ten  to  the sound  of  the  mu - sic,
Lis - ten  to  the sound  of  the  mu - sic,

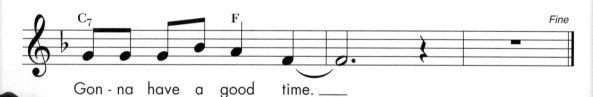

Gon - na  have  a  good  time. ____

**Web Site** Go to *www.sbgmusic.com* to find out more about Rosenshontz.

**REFRAIN**

C
Come on, let's go, one, two, three;
Come on, let's go, sev'n, eight, nine;

F ... C7 ... F
You're the on - ly one so dance _ with me;
When you dance with me, I feel ___ so fine;

C ... C7 ... F
Come on, let's go, four, five, six;
Come on, let's go, ten, 'leven, twelve;

*D.C. al Fine*

C ... C7
If you don't dance, I'm in a fix. ___
If you don't dance, I'll dance my - self. ___

3.  Listen to the sound of the saxophone,
    Listen to the sound of the beat!
    Listen to the sound of the saxophone,
    Gonna have a good time!
    *(Fine)*

# LOUD AND SOFT SOUNDS = DYNAMICS!

Music around us can be loud or soft. Look at the pictures below. Imagine the sounds you might hear. Describe the **dynamics** to a partner.

**Dynamics** is a word that describes the loudness or softness of music.

# Using Dynamics

**Listen** to the loud and soft parts in this song.

Now **sing** the song.

# Heigh-Ho

from *Snow White and the Seven Dwarfs*

Words by Larry Morey

Music by Frank Churchill

"Heigh-ho, heigh-ho," To make your trou-bles go,
ho, heigh-ho," It's home from work we go,

just keep on sing-ing all day long "Heigh-ho,
(whistle or hum) _____ "Heigh-ho,

heigh-ho, heigh-ho, heigh-ho, heigh-ho,"
heigh-ho, heigh-ho, heigh-ho, heigh-ho,"

For if you're feel-ing low, You pos-i-tive-ly can't go wrong
All sev-en in a row, (whistle or hum) _____

1.
With a "heigh, heigh-ho heigh-ho, heigh-
2.
With a "heigh, heigh- -ho."

# THE BEAT GOES ON

Most music has a **steady beat.** There are many ways to keep the beat. As you **listen** to the song, **clap** to keep the beat.

A **steady beat** is the regular pulse found in most music.

1–5

Time to Sing

*Words and Music by Raffi, D. Pike, and B. & B. Simpson*

VERSE G
1. It's time to sing a song or two.

Am7 D7
You with me and me with you. ___

Last time to Coda
G E7 Am7 D7 G
Time for us to sing a - while, . Hey, hey, hey.

REFRAIN
C C#dim G
And it's time for say - ing hi and hel - lo.

A7 D7 D.C. al Coda
Let's all sing a song that we know.

8

Coda

Am₇  D₇  G  E₇  Am₇  D₇  G  E₇

Hey, hey, hey, I'm sing-ing, Hey, hey, hey, we're sing-ing

Am₇  D₇  G

Hey, _____ hey, ___ hey, ___ hey.

2. It's time for us to clap our hands
   in rhythm with the beat.
   Time for hands to clap awhile,
   Hey, hey, hey. *Refrain*

3. It's time for us to tap our toes
   together with our feet.
   Time for toes to tap awhile,
   Hey, hey, hey. *Refrain*

4. It's time to make a sound you like,
   la la la . . . .
   *Refrain, then repeat Verse 1 to Coda*

## Moving to the Beat

**Move** to show the steady
beat as you **sing** the
song. How many different
ways can you keep a
steady beat?

## Rhythm of the Words

Music has steady beats. It also has **rhythm. Clap** the rhythm of the words of "Time to Sing."

## Tap Dance Rhythms

Tap dancers make exciting rhythms with their feet. They wear special shoes with metal tips at the toes and heels.

Liam Burke is a member of *Tap Dogs*. **Listen** to the rhythm of his tap dancing.

**1–7**
**Interview with Liam Burke**

### MUSIC MAKERS

## TAP DOGS

*Tap Dogs* is a stage show from Australia. It is part tap dance and part rock concert. The dancers wear work boots. They dance on steel, on wood floors, and on electronic drum pads.

# Get the Rhythm

**Sing** this song as you **pat** the steady beat. **Sing** the song again and **clap** the rhythm of the words.

 1–8

### GO AROUND THE CORN, SALLY

*African American Work Song*

Go a-round, round and round, Go a-round the corn, Sal-ly.

Hey now, Hey __ now, Go a-round the corn, Sal-ly.

Fast-er still, Fast-er still, Round and round the corn, Sal-ly.

All a-round, all a-round, Go a-round the corn, Sal-ly.

Find a partner. One claps the rhythm as the other pats a steady beat. Sometimes one claps two times when the other pats only once.

## One and Two Sounds on a Beat

**Tap** the corn as you **say** the words.

> Go  a  -  round,    'round  and    'round

The notes below show the rhythm. **Tap** the rhythm.

Go  a  -  round,    'round  and    'round

Find the ears of corn that have one sound.

> One sound on a beat

Then find the ears of corn that have two sounds.

> Two sounds on a beat

# Rhythms at Rest

**Listen** to this song from China. At the end of each line, there is one beat with no sound.

1–10

## Xiao yin chuan
### (Silver Moon Boat)

*Folk Song from China*

Yue    er    wan wan xiang    yi    tiao chuan    gua    tian shang
Lit - tle    sil - ver moon    rides    the    sky    like    a    boat,

Chuan guo  xing xing    ta    yi    ran    qing    ying piao dang
Past    the    twink-ling stars    it    will    float,    light - ly    float.

Yang    fan ___    xiang    zhe    xi    fang    hang
Sail,    lit - tle    moon    boat,    to    the    west,

Jia    xiao xiao  yin    chuan    duo    an    xiang.
Sail,    lit - tle    moon    boat,    while    I    rest.

## No Sound on the Beat

Find these rhythms in the song.
- One sound on the beat = ♩
- Two sounds on the beat = ♫
- No sounds on the beat = 𝄽

**rest**

Find the sailboat below with the 𝄽.

Jia   xiao xiao   yin   chuan

duo   an   xiang

Now **play** this pattern as you sing the song.

Rhythm Fun!

This little bird from Spain sings a special song.
Find what the bird sings. Then **tap** the rhythm.

1–14

## Un pajarito
### (A Little Bird)

English Words by Alice Firgau

Folk Song from Spain

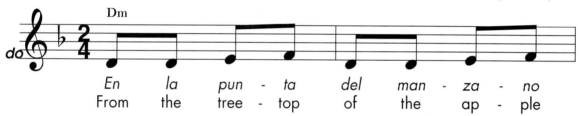

En    la    pun - ta    del    man - za - no
From   the    tree - top    of    the    ap - ple

hay   un   pa - ja - ri - to,   un   pa - ja - ri - to,
tree   a   lit - tle   bird   sings,   A   lit - tle   bird   sings,

que   sin   ce - sar   siem - pre   can - ta a - sì.
Sings   al - ways sweet - ly   the   whole   day   long.

Chi - ru - li - ru - li!   Chi - ru - li - ru - li

can - ta, pa - ja - ri - to, can - ta y siem - pre can - ta a - sì.
Lit - tle   bird, come sing your song, so   sweet - ly   all   day long.

## Rhythm Patterns

**Sing** the song again. Find this rhythm pattern in the song.

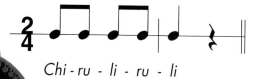

Chi - ru - li - ru - li

> **Rhythm syllables** are used to name specific rhythmic units.

Using **rhythm syllables, say** the pattern. What other patterns can you find in the song?

## Show What You Know!

These rhythm patterns are from songs you know. First **clap** or **pat** each pattern. Then name the song.

1.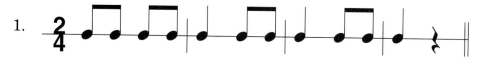

2.

3.

**Create** your own rhythm pattern using ♩, ♫, and 𝄽.

**Clap** or **pat** your pattern. **Play** it on an instrument.

# Let the Spirit MOVE you

## Listen to "Michael, Row the Boat Ashore."

 1-18

### Michael, Row the Boat Ashore

*African American Spiritual*

*Call*

1. Mi - chael, row   the   boat   a - shore,
2. Sis - ter   help   to   trim   the   sail,

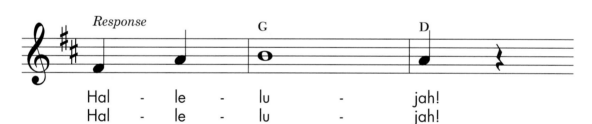

*Response*

Hal - le - lu - jah!
Hal - le - lu - jah!

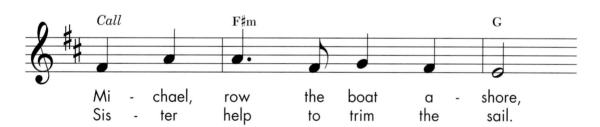

*Call*

Mi - chael, row   the   boat   a - shore,
Sis - ter   help   to   trim   the   sail.

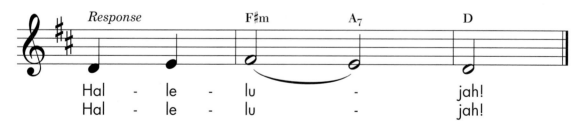

*Response*

Hal - le - lu - jah!
Hal - le - lu - jah!

3. River Jordan's deep and wide, . . .   4. Trumpet sound the jubilee, . . .
   Milk and honey on the other side. . . .      Cross this riv'r and we'll be free. . . .

## Call and Response

Did you notice that first one person sings the **call,** then a group sings the **response?**

**Call and response** is a style of choral singing. First one person sings the call. Then the rest of the chorus sings a response, or an answer.

## Get in the Boat and Move!

Take your place in the "boat" and **sing** the song. Use your rhythm sticks as oars during the call parts. **Tap** the floor on the beat.

During the response raise the sticks into the air. **Tap** them together as you sway from side to side on the beat.

# Up and Down the Music Trail

Cowboys spent long days and nights moving cattle along the dusty trail. They sang songs to make their work easier. They also sang to pass the time in the evenings.

**Sing** this cowboy song. Find the high and low **pitches.**

**Pitch** is another word for a musical note. Pitch is how high or low a note sounds.

1-20

## Lone Star Trail

*Cowboy Song from the United States*

**VERSE**

1. I start-ed on the trail on June twen-ty-third,

I been punch-in' Tex-as cat-tle on the Lone Star Trail;

**REFRAIN**

Sing-in' ki yi yip-pi yip-pi yay, yip-pi yay!

Sing-in' ki yi yip-pi yip-pi yay! _____

2. I'm up in the mornin' before daylight,
   And before I sleep the moon shines bright. *Refrain*

3. Oh, it's bacon and beans 'most every day,
   I'd as soon be a-eatin' prairie hay. *Refrain*

4. My feet are in the stirrups and my rope is on the side,
   Show me a horse that I can't ride. *Refrain*

## Moving High, Moving Low

**Listen** to "Lone Star Trail."

**Move** up and down to show the high and low pitches. Pretend you are riding a horse.

## Play Along

Now **play** these patterns while the class sings.

# Aaron Copland

**Aaron Copland** (1900–1990) was an American composer whose music is very popular. He began writing songs when he was eight years old. He started writing an opera when he was only eleven.

# Cowboys on Holiday

**Listen** to *Buckaroo Holiday* as you follow the listening map. The knots on the rope show how the pitches move from high to low.

1–21
## Buckaroo Holiday

**from *Rodeo***
**by Aaron Copland**

Imagine the cowboys celebrating at a rodeo after a very long cattle drive.

*Buckaroo Holiday*
**Listening Map**

# Follow the Direction

**Listen** to "My Father's House."
Trace the direction of the **melody.**

**Melody** is a row of pitches that move up or down or repeat.

Won't you come
with
me _____ to my
fa-
ther's
house, _____

To my fa-
ther's
house, _____
house,
to my fa-
ther's
house? _____

Won't you come
with
me _____ to my
fa-
ther's
house, _____

There
is
peace, _____
peace, _____
peace. _____

# of the MUSIC

Now **sing** the song. **Move** your hand
to show the direction of the melody.

**1–22**

## My Father's House

*Traditional Song from the Southern United States*

1.–3.    Won't you come with me    to    my    fa-ther's house,

To    my    fa-ther's house,    to    my    fa-ther's house?

Won't you    come with    me    to    my    fa - ther's house,

1. There    is    peace,    peace,    peace.
2. There    is    joy,    joy,    joy.
3. There    is    love,    love,    love.

# Three Pitches

"Lucy Locket" is a singing game. The song has only the three pitches—*so, mi,* and *la.*

These are the hand signs.

so          mi          la

# Singing with Pitch Syllables

The first pitch of the song is *so*. **Sing** "Lucy Locket" with **pitch syllables.** Then add the hand signs.

**Pitch syllables** are used to name pitches, for example, *so*, *mi*, and *la*.

**1–25**

# Lucy Locket

*Street Rhyme*

Lu - cy Lock - et  lost her pock - et.  Kit - ty Fish - er found  it.

Not  a  pen - ny  was there in  it.  On - ly  rib - bon 'round  it.

Pitches are written on a five-line staff.

**staff**

Sometimes *so*, *mi*, and *la* are in different places on the staff. On this staff, *so* is in the third space.

Where are *mi* and *la*?

# Read Pizza, Play Pizza

Find *so, mi,* and *la* in "Pizza, Pizza, Daddy-o."

 1–26

## Pizza, Pizza, Daddy-o

*Singing Game from the United States*

*Solo*
C

so

Jim - my's got a girl - friend,

*Chorus*
C          *Solo*
Am  3   G   Am

Piz - za, piz - za, Dad-dy-o,   How do you know   it?

*Chorus*
C          *Solo*
Am   G   Am

Piz - za, piz - za, Dad-dy-o,   'Cause he told   me,

*Chorus*
C          *Solo*
Am   G   Am

Piz - za, piz - za, Dad-dy-o,   Let's rope   it,

◀ *Children Playing London Bridge* by William H. Johnson

"London Bridge," like "Pizza, Pizza, Daddy-o," is a singing game. Children play games like these in playgrounds, in schoolyards, and on sidewalks.

rope it, rope __ it, Dad - dy - o, Let's swim it,

swim it, swim __ it, Dad - dy - o, Let's duck it,

duck it, duck __ it, Dad - dy - o, Let's twist it,

twist it, twist __ it, Dad - dy - o, Let's end it,

End it, end __ it, Dad - dy - o.

# The Pizza Pizza Game

Play this game as you **sing** "Pizza, Pizza, Daddy-o." First the leader sings. Then the whole group answers.

You can **create** your own verses for this game.

Beat 1   Beat 2   Beat 3   Beat 4

Hold beat 6 position.

Beat 5   Beat 6   Beat 7   Beat 8

Remember that *so, mi,* and *la* can be in different places on the staff. On the staff below, *so* is in the third space. Where are *mi* and *la*?

Show where each of these pitch syllable patterns would go on a staff. Start with *so* in the third space.

1.

*so   so   la   la   so   mi*

2.

*so   so   mi   la   so   so*

# You Are the Music

You can make music without an instrument.
**Listen** carefully to "Down, Down, Baby."
Which sounds are like instruments but really
performed with parts of the body?

When you make music like this, it is called
body percussion.

## Down, Down, Baby

*African American Clapping Song*

1. Down, down, ba - by, down,___ down a rol - ler coast - er,

Sweet, sweet ba - by, I ___ love a rol - ler coast - er;

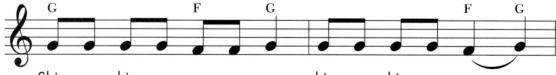

Shim - my, shim - my, co - coa pop, shim - my, shim - my, pop, ___

All to - geth - er with the chick - ens and the feath - ers.

Warren Smith is a musician and hambone artist.
Hamboning is a style of body percussion. ▼

P - O - P spells pop, oh, my hon - ey,

P - O - P spells pop, oh, my ba - by,

P - O - P spells POP!

2. Down, down, baby, down, down a roller coaster,
Sweet, sweet baby, I love a roller coaster;
Shimmy, shimmy, cocoa pop, shimmy, shimmy pop.
Grandma, Grandmama, sick in bed,
Called the doctor and the doctor said,
"Let's get the motion of the head, ding dong,
Let's get the motion of the hands, clap clap,
Let's get the motion of the feet, stomp stomp,
Put it all together and what do you get?
Ding dong, clap clap, stomp stomp.
Say it all backwards and what do you get?
Stomp stomp, clap clap, ding dong!"

# Thin to Thick

**Perform** this rhyme to a steady beat.

**RIDDLE REE**

*Words and Rhythmic Setting by Grace Nash*

1-29

Rid - dle, rid - dle, rid - dle, ree, do what I do af - ter me.

Stamp, clap, stamp, clap. Sway, sway.

Touch your toes, touch your nose, 'round in cir - cles each one goes.

Bow once, bow twice, bend down low and plant some rice.

Lift your hands up to the sky, shake them out and hold them high.

Clap your hands, stamp your feet, cym - bals crash and that's com - plete!

## Adding Sounds

Add this **ostinato** as the class performs "Riddle Ree."

> An **ostinato** is a short repeated pattern.

Rid - dle me this and rid - dle me that!

Then add this ostinato.

Slide slide to the far side.

When one person speaks alone, the sound is thin. When more people join in, the sound gets thicker.

RIBIT, RIBIT RIBIT

Chirp, Chirp

# Putting It

**1.** Read the notation for "Lucy Locket" on page 27.

    **a.** Find four words in the song that are sung on *so*.

    **b.** Find four words that are sung on *la*.

    **c.** Find three words that are sung on *mi*.

**2.** Match the following musical terms with their definitions.

    **a.** steady beat    • a pattern of long and short sounds and silences

    **b.** ostinato    • the regular pulse found in most music

    **c.** rhythm    • a short repeated pattern

1–31

## What Do You Hear? 1

Listen for the drum in each of the four examples. Is it playing the steady beat or the rhythm?

**1.**     steady beat       rhythm

**2.**     steady beat       rhythm

**3.**     steady beat       rhythm

**4.**     steady beat       rhythm

# All Together

## What You Can Do

### Play a Rhythm

As the teacher plays a steady beat, tap this rhythm in the palm of your hand.

### Create a Rhythm

Create a body percussion part to play as you sing "Lone Star Trail." Start by imitating the sound of horses' hooves. Use only 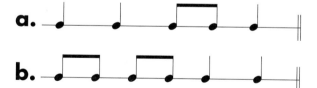, and ♩.

### Create a Melody

Work with a partner to create your own call-and-response song.

- Clap each of the rhythms below.

  **a.**

  **b.**

- Use *so, mi,* and *la* to create a melody to go with each rhythm.

- Perform one melody as a call while your partner performs the other melody as the response.

# Dance to the Music

What different ways do you explore music? Some music makes you want to dance. **Listen** to *Liberty/Chicken Reel* and identify when the music changes. Then **move** to the music. **Create** movements that show when the music changes.

**1–35**
## Liberty/Chicken Reel

**Traditional**

Some of the instruments you will hear are pennywhistle, fiddle, and hammered dulcimer.

# Exploring Music

## A Rockin' Rhythm
**Sing** and **move** to this song.

1–36

# The Music's in Me

*Words and Music by Jill Gallina*

VERSE

1. When I hear mu - sic, mu-sic with a rock-in' beat, _
2. When I hear mu - sic, mu-sic with a rock-in' beat, _

my hands start clap - pin', my toes start tap - pin',
my heart starts thump - in', my blood starts pump - in',

I've got-ta move my feet. _
I've got-ta move my feet. _

I love that rhy - thm.
I love that rhy - thm.

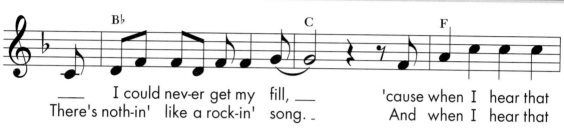

___ I could nev-er get my fill, ___ 'cause when I hear that
There's noth-in' like a rock-in' song. _ And when I hear that

mu - sic play, _ you know that I just can't sit still. __
mu - sic play, _ you know I've got - ta sing a - long __

**REFRAIN**

The mu-sic's in me. _ It keeps me rock-in' you see. _

The mu-sic's in me. _ It keeps me rock-in' you see. _

## Creating Music

**Listen** to the song again. Then **create** a rhythm pattern to play along with the recording. What instrument will you **play**?

# "Speed Up, Slow Down"

**Sing** "Miss Mary Mack" at different speeds, or **tempos.**

**Tempo** is the speed of the beat in music.

1–38

## Miss Mary Mack

*African American Clapping Game Song*

1. Miss Ma - ry Mack, Mack, Mack,

All dressed in black, black, black,

With sil - ver but-tons, but-tons, but-tons,

All down her back, back, back.

2. She asked her mother,
   mother, mother,
   For fifteen cents, cents, cents,
   To see the elephants,
      elephants, elephants
   Jump over the fence, fence, fence.

3. They jumped so high,
      high, high,
   They touched the sky, sky, sky,
   And never came down,
      down, down,
   'Til the fourth of July, 'ly, 'ly.

## Game Time

Play this game with a partner.

Step 4

1. Cross your arms, hands on shoulders.

2. Pat your thighs.

3. Clap your hands.

4. Clap your partner's right hand.

Step 8

5. Clap your hands.

6. Clap your partner's left hand.

7. Clap your hands.

8. Clap both of your partner's hands.

## *Arts* **Connection**

▲ *Untitled* by Keith Haring (1958–1990). Haring created bright, exciting paintings. How does this painting show movement?

# Playing with Rhythms

**Sing** this game song from Trinidad. **Listen** for the sound of the steel drums on the recording.

## Gypsy in the Moonlight

2-1

*Folk Song from Trinidad*

1. Gyp - sy    in    the  moon - light,   Gyp - sy    in    the  dew,
2. Walk in, gyp - sy, walk   in,    Walk right  in    I    say,

Gyp - sy   ne - ver  come  back un - til   the  clock strikes two.
Walk in - to   my  par - lor   to  hear the  ban - jo   play.

3. I don't want nobody,
   Nobody wants me,
   All I want is Mary
   to come and dance with me.

4. Tra-la-la . . .

**Say and tap** these rhythms.
Then find them in the song.

1

2

## Speaking Rhythms

**Perform** "Alligator Pie."

Find a rhythm pattern that is the same as a pattern from "Gypsy in the Moonlight." Is it 1 or 2?

**2–3**

# Alligator Pie

*Poem by Dennis Lee*

*Rhythmic Setting by Edith Bicknell*

Al - li - ga - tor pie, al - li - ga - tor pie,

If I don't get some I think I'm gon - na die.

Give a - way the green grass, give a - way the sky, But

don't give a - way my al - li - ga - tor pie.

Pick a

**Sing** "Four in a Boat." Which lines have the same rhythm pattern?

# Four in a Boat

2–5

*Play-Party Song from Appalachia*

1. Four in a boat and the tide rolls high,

Four in a boat and the tide rolls high,

Four in a boat and the tide rolls high,

Wait-ing for a pret-ty one to come bye and bye.

2. Choose your partner and stay all day, . . .
   We don't care what the old folks say.

3. Eight in a boat and it won't go 'round, . . .
   Swing that pretty one that you just found.

# Pattern

## Play a Pattern!

Say this rhythm pattern using rhythm syllables.
Then **play** the rhythm on an instrument.

# Rhythm in Art

Find the patterns in this painting. Why do you think it is called *Rhythmical*?

*Arts* **Connection**

▲ *Rhythmical* by Paul Klee (1879–1940)

# Piano Patterns

**Listen** to *Allegro non troppo* by Béla Bartók.
Find two rhythm patterns that are different.
**Move** to show the patterns.

2–9

**Allegro non troppo, no. 33**

**from *For Children, Volume II*
by Béla Bartók**

Bártok wrote these pieces especially for young children
to play on the piano.

## Show What You Know!

**Clap** these rhythms. Find the patterns
that repeat.

1.

2.

3.

4.

# Get on the BEAT

**Sing** this song. Try to *step it down* on the **strong beats.**

The **strong beat** is the most important beat in a rhythm pattern.

 2–10

## Way Down in the Schoolyard

*Traditional
New Words and Musical Arrangement
by Sharon, Lois, and Bram*

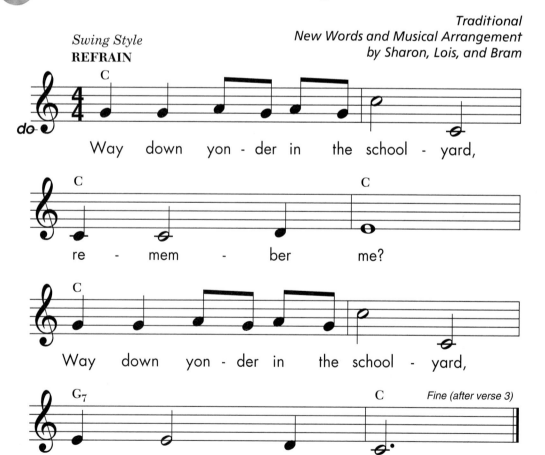

*Swing Style*
**REFRAIN**

do

Way down yon- der in the school - yard,

re - mem - ber me?

Way down yon - der in the school - yard,

*Fine (after verse 3)*

re - mem - ber me.

# Move It, Groove It!

**Listen** to the original version of the song.
**Move** on the strong beats.

**2-12**

## Way Down Yonder in the Brickyard

**Traditional African American**

Bessie Jones and the Georgia Sea Island Singers
made this recording in 1979.

**VERSE**

1. Well  step  it,  step  it,  step  it ___  down, _

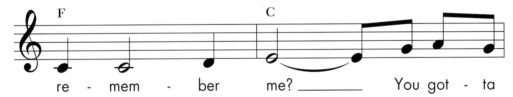

re - mem - ber  me? _____  You got - ta

step  it,  step  it,  step  it ___  down, _

re - mem - ber  me.

2. Now twirl your sweetheart, twirl her (him) now,
   Remember me?
   You gotta twirl your sweetheart, twirl him (her) now,
   Remember me.  *(Repeat)*
   *Refrain*

3. Now find another, find him (her) now,
   Remember me?
   You gotta find another, find him (her) now,
   Remember me.  *(Repeat)*
   *Refrain*

# SINGIN' THE BLUES

The blues is a way for people to express their feelings through music. **Sing** this blues song with feeling.

**Form** is the order of same and different ideas in music.

"Good Mornin', Blues" has two different musical ideas, **a** and **b**. The order of these ideas is called **form.** What is the form of this song?

2-13

## GOOD MORNIN', BLUES

Edited and New Additional Material by Alan Lomax

New Words and New Music Arranged by Huddie Ledbetter

1. Good morn - in', blues, Blues, how do you do?

Good morn - in', blues, Blues, how do you do?

I'm do-in' all right, ___ Good morn-in', how are you?

2. Called yesterday, Here you come today,
   Called yesterday, Here you come today.
   Your mouth's wide open but you don't know what to say.

# HUDDIE LEDBETTER

Huddie "Leadbelly" Ledbetter (1885–1949) was a well-known blues singer and guitar player. Leadbelly is in the Blues Hall of Fame *and* the Rock and Roll Hall of Fame.

## Can't Get Enough of the Blues

**Listen** to the melody of this blues song. It is sung by Huddie Ledbetter. Is it in **a** **a** **b** form?

2-15

**When a Man's a Long Way from Home**

**Traditional Blues Song**

Huddie Ledbetter said he could sing and play more than 500 different songs.

# Singing Ecuador

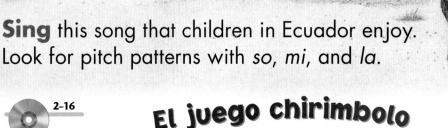

**Sing** this song that children in Ecuador enjoy. Look for pitch patterns with *so*, *mi*, and *la*.

2–16

## El juego chirimbolo
### (The *Chirimbolo* Game)

English Words by Alice Firgau                    Singing Game from Ecuador

do-

El jue - go chi - rim - bo - lo, ¡qué bo - ni - to es!
This game is chi - rim - bo - lo; Play and you'll have fun.

Con un pie, o - tro pie, u - na ma - no, o - tra ma - no,
First one foot, oth - er foot; Then one hand, __ oth - er hand; __

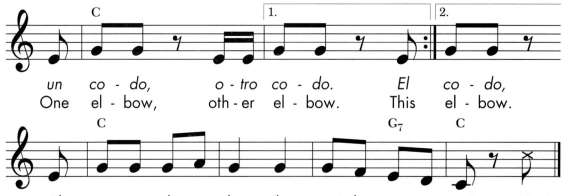

un co - do, o - tro co - do. El co - do,
One el - bow, oth - er el - bow. This el - bow.

El jue - go chi - rim - bo - lo, ¡qué bo - ni - to es! ¡Hey!
We're play - ing chi - rim - bo - lo. Now the game is done. Hey!

# Play a Game

Play the *chirimbolo* game with classmates.
The words of the song tell you how to move.

Ecuador is a country
on the continent of
South America. ▶

Ecuador

South
America

**Video Library** Watch *Singing Games*. This
video shows singing games from the United
States, Mexico, Japan, and Ghana.

# Find a New Pitch

**Sing** this song using *so*, *mi*, and *la*.
**Listen** for a new pitch at the end.
Is the new pitch higher or lower
than *so*, *mi*, and *la*?

2–21

## Clouds of Gray

*Words and Music by Katinka S. Daniel*

la

so

mi

1. Clouds of gray are in the sky,
2. Lit - tle flow - ers down - ward creep,

Flocks of birds are pass - ing by,
Nod their drow - sy heads and sleep,

Trees now dress in fad - ed brown,
All the world must say "good night,"

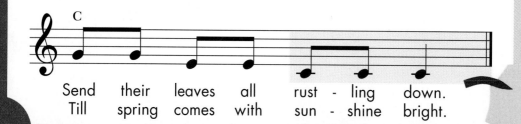

Send their leaves all rust - ling down.
Till spring comes with sun - shine bright.

?

la     so     mi     ?

## New Pitch—New Sign

As you **sing** the song, show hand signs for *la*, *so*, *mi*, and the new pitch. Hum the new pitch.

## Sing an Autumn Poem

Try singing this poem, using the melody from "Clouds of Gray."

### Wind Has Shaken Autumn Down
*by Tony Johnston*

Wind has shaken autumn down,
left it sprawling on the ground,
shawling all in gold below,
waiting for the hush of snow.

# NAME THE NEW PITCH

**Sing** this moon song. Find *so* and *mi* on the staff. *So* and *mi* are in spaces. Where is the new pitch?

2–23

## I SEE THE MOON

*Melody by Denise Bacon, Adapted*

do

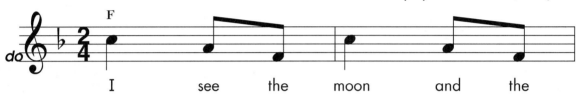

I see the moon and the

moon sees me.

Moon sees some - bod - y

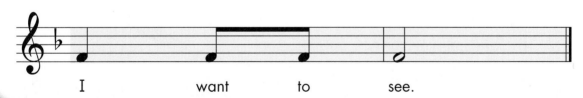

I want to see.

# What Is the Name?

The new pitch is called *do*.

**Sing** *"I See the Moon,"* using *so*, *mi*, and *do*.
Point to each pitch on the staff.

## Show What You Know!

**Sing** these patterns using pitch syllables.

1. *do*

2. *do*

3. *do*

**Tune In**

Sometimes the moon seems very large and close. It is really more than 230,000 miles from earth.

# MELODIC

Every melody moves in its own direction.
**Sing** this song and trace the path of the melody.

2-25

## Down the Ohio

*River Shanty*

**VERSE**

*do*

The riv-er is up and the chan-nel is deep,

The wind is stead-y and strong.

1. Oh, won't we have a jol-ly good time
2. The waves do splash from shore ___ to shore

As we go sail-ing a-long.

# PATHWAYS

## Follow the Path of a Melody

Find where the pitches repeat,
where the pitches skip,
and where the pitches step.

**REFRAIN**

G                                           C

Down    the    riv - er,    Oh,    down    the    riv - er,

D₇                                          G

Oh,    down    the    riv - er    we    go. _____

G                                           C

Down    the    riv - er,    Oh,    down    the    riv - er,

D₇                                          G

Oh,    down    the    O - hi - o!

**CD-ROM** Create your own melody with *Making Music* software. Use steps, skips, and repeated pitches.

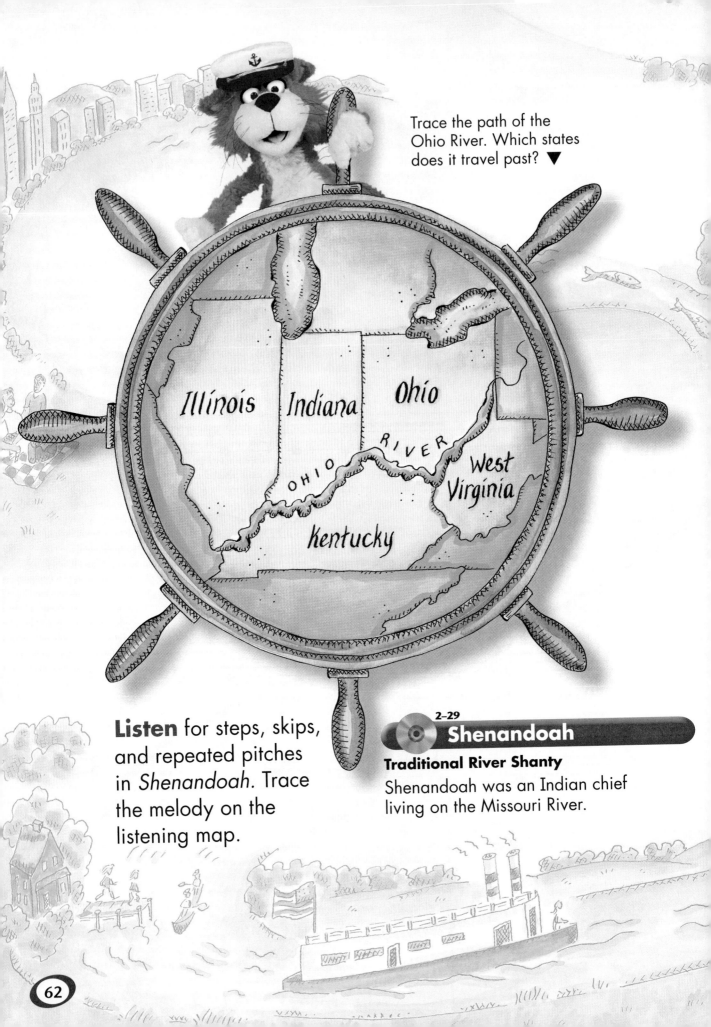

Trace the path of the Ohio River. Which states does it travel past? ▼

Illinois Indiana Ohio

OHIO RIVER

West Virginia

Kentucky

**Listen** for steps, skips, and repeated pitches in *Shenandoah*. Trace the melody on the listening map.

2–29
## Shenandoah

**Traditional River Shanty**

Shenandoah was an Indian chief living on the Missouri River.

# shenandoah Listening Map

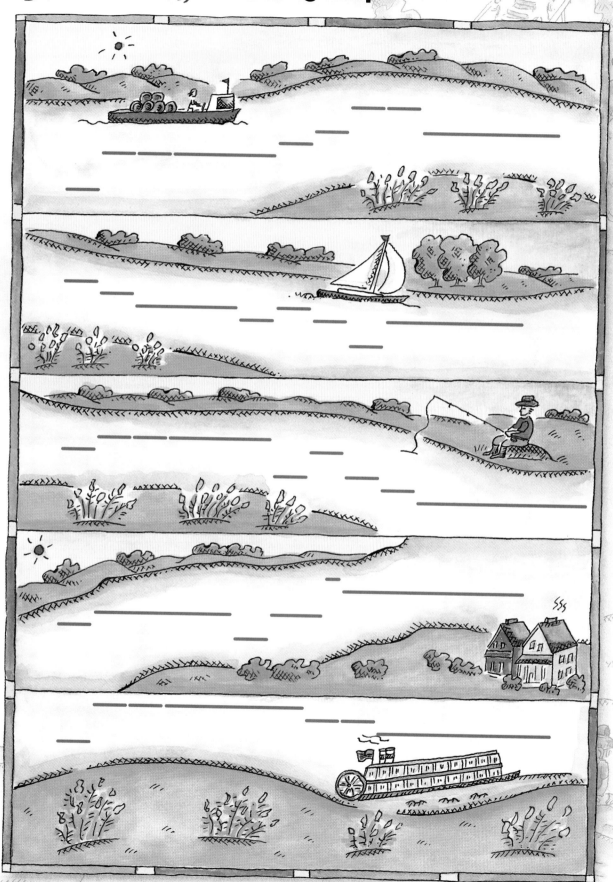

# Percussion

The way an instrument is made gives it a special sound, or **timbre.**

**Sing** this song from Israel. **Listen** for the timbre of the tambourine.

**Timbre** is the special sound each instrument makes.

2–30

# Achshav
## (Awake! Awake!)

*English Words by David Eddleman*

*Folk Song from Israel*

G
do

D7

Ach - shav, ach - shav, b' - em - ek Yis - ra - el;
A - wake! A - wake! the val - leys of our land,

D7

G

Ach - shav, ach - shav, b' - em - ek Yis - ra - el.
A - wake! A - wake! the val - leys of our land.

G

D7

Tum - ba, tum - ba, tum - ba, b' - em - ek Yis - ra - el, Hey!
Tum - ba, tum - ba, tum - ba, the land of Is - ra - el, Hey!

D7

G

Tum - ba, tum - ba, tum - ba, b' - em - ek Yis - ra - el, Hey!
Tum - ba, tum - ba, tum - ba, the land of Is - ra - el, Hey!

# Timbres

## Tambourine Techniques

Tambourines are played using different **techniques.** They can be tapped or shaken. **Play** these tambourine patterns with "Achshav."

**Technique** is the special skill used to play an instrument.

(val - leys    of    our    land)

(shake)

(Is - ra - el,    Hey!)

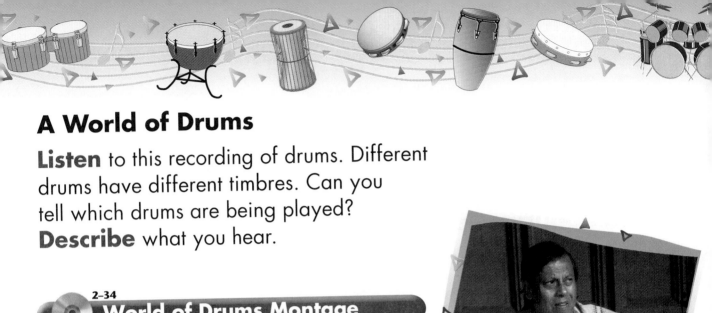

# A World of Drums

**Listen** to this recording of drums. Different drums have different timbres. Can you tell which drums are being played? **Describe** what you hear.

**2–34**
**World of Drums Montage**

▲ Tabla player from India

▲ Timpani player

▼ *Taiko* drum players

▲ Drum set player

# Who Is the Drum?

**Listen** to this poem.
Who is the narrator
of the poem?

2–35
**De Beat**

**by Grace Nichols**
The poet is a native of British Guiana.

▲ *Djembe* player

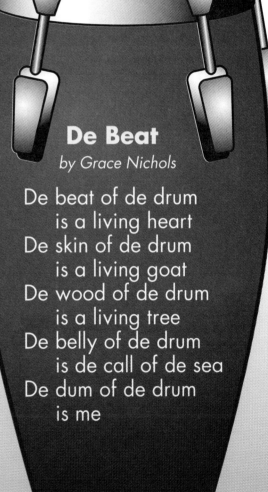

## De Beat
*by Grace Nichols*

De beat of de drum
    is a living heart
De skin of de drum
    is a living goat
De wood of de drum
    is a living tree
De belly of de drum
    is de call of de sea
De dum of de drum
    is me

# Speaking in Layers

Children in West Africa learn to drum when they are about seven years old. They chant words to help them learn the patterns.

Combine these names of African tribes in different ways. Say the names over and over in rhythm. This **creates** an ostinato.

*Ibo*      *Ashanti*    *Hausa*
*Fon*      *Yoruba*     *Kotokoli*

## Performing in Layers

**Perform** your ostinato with the ostinato of a classmate. **Create** a thicker sound by adding more ostinatos.

## Hear the Layers

**Listen** for the layers of repeating patterns in *Oya*.

2–36
**Oya**

**from *Primitive Fire*
by Babatunde Olatunji**

Some of the instruments you will hear are *shekere*, *gankogui*, and *djembe*.

## M·U·S·I·C  M·A·K·E·R·S

### Babatunde Olatunji

**Babatunde Olatunji** (born 1927) is a well-known drummer from Nigeria. In the 1960s he brought the sounds of Nigerian drumming and chanting to the United States.

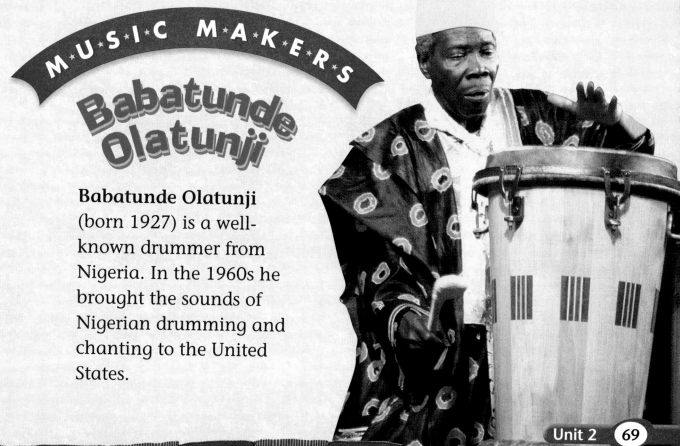

# Play a Musical Message

**Sing** this story song from Ghana. Ghana is a country in West Africa.

Ayelivi is a girl who goes to pick berries for her mother and gets lost in the jungle. The friendly animals help her find her way home.

### Ayelivi

*Story Song from Ghana*
*Arranged by Komla Amoaku*

A - ye - li - vi ___ no ku - do mi do
A - ye - li - vi ___ has lost her way and

ba ba ___ n'a - ye - li - vi.
can't find ___ her moth - er dear.

Yie yie mi do ba ba ___ n'a - ye - li - vi.
Wah, wah, we feel sad for ___ A - ye - li - vi.

# Building Texture

**Play** these rhythms one at a time. Then play them together in layers to create a thicker **texture.**

**Texture** is how thin or thick the music sounds.

| | | | | | | | |
|---|---|---|---|---|---|---|---|
| 1 | 2 | | 4 | 5 | | 7 | 8 |
| 1 | | 3 | | 5 | | 7 | |
| | 2 | | 4 | | 6 | | 8 |
| ↓ | ↑ | ↓ | ↑ | ↓ | ↑ | ↓ | ↑ |

## Perform the Story

**Play** your music with the story about Ayelivi.

**Tune In**

Story songs are used throughout Africa. They teach children important lessons about life.

# Putting It

## What Do You Know?

**1.** How do the pitches below move? Match the music with the correct word.

**a.** • step

**b.** • repeated pitches

**c.** • skip

**2.** Name the pitches in the staff below.

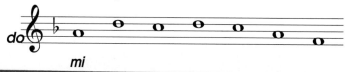

do

mi

## 2–41
## What Do You Hear? 2

You will hear three pairs of musical examples. Decide which word or phrase best describes each example.

**1. a.** fast      slow
    **b.** fast      slow

**2. a.** loud      soft
    **b.** loud      soft

**3. a.** getting faster      getting slower
    **b.** getting faster      getting slower

# All Together

What You Can Do

## Sing the Blues

Sing "Good Mornin', Blues." Create a new verse in **a** **a** **b** form.

## Play Rhythms

Tap each of the following rhythms four times in the palm of your hand.

a.

b.

c.

Choose an instrument and play the same rhythms again along with the recording of *"Ayelivi."*

## Create a Rhythm

Compose a new 8-beat rhythm pattern using ♩, ♫, and 𝄽. Play your pattern for the class.

# Let's Get Steppin'!

**Move** with energy. Show the strong beats.

## Step in Time

*Words and Music by Richard M. and Robert B. Sherman*

1. Kick your knees up, step in time!
2. Spin a - bout and step in time!

Kick your knees up, step in time!
Spin a - bout and step in time!

Nev - er need a rea - son, nev - er need a rhyme,

Kick your knees up, step in time!
Spin a - bout and step in time!

3. Link your elbows, step in time! . . .
4. 'Round the circle, step in time! . . .
5. Flap like a birdie, step in time! . . .
6. Step in time, step in time! . . .

# Learning the Language of MUSIC

# Ragtime Beats

Ragtime is a style of music with strong beats in unexpected places. **Listen** to this ragtime piano piece. **Move** to show the stronger beats.

3–1
## The Entertainer

**by Scott Joplin**

Scott Joplin was the most famous composer of ragtime music. The U.S. Postal Service even put Joplin's picture on a postage stamp!

# Accents!

Say this poem in rhythm. Add **accents** to give it some pizzazz.

An **accent** gives extra importance to a note in a rhythm pattern.

An **accent** on a note looks like this. →

 3–4

## Boogie Chant and Dance

*Street Rhyme*

Ladies and gentlemen and children too,
These dancin' kids gonna boogie for you.
They're gonna turn all around,
They're gonna touch the ground,
They're gonna shake their shoulders
Till the sun goes down.
Hands up! Ha-ha, Ha-ha-ha!
Hands down! Ha-ha, Ha-ha-ha!
Got a penny, call Jack Benny. Ha-ha, Ha-ha-ha!
Got a nickel, buy a pickle. Ha-ha, Ha-ha-ha!
Got a dime, life is fine. Ha-ha, Ha-ha-ha!

## Perform with Accents

Find the notes that have accents in "Two Little Sausages." **Move** to show the accents as you listen to the recording.

Then say the rhyme with accents on the right words.

3-6

# Two Little Sausages

*Traditional Jump-Rope Rhyme*

Two lit - tle sau - sag - es fry - ing in a pan,

One went POP! and the oth - er went BLAM!

# Hear a New Rhythm

**Listen** to "Tideo" and **move** to the beat. Do you hear a new rhythm in the song that is not , or ? Which words have the new rhythm?

3–8

## Tideo

*Play-Party Song from Texas*

Pass one win-dow Ti - de - o,   Pass two win-dows Ti - de - o,

Pass three win-dows Ti - de - o,   Jin-gle at the win-dow  Ti - de - o.

Ti - de - o,   Ti - de - o,   Jin-gle at the win-dow  Ti - de - o.

## See a New Rhythm

**Tap** the rhythms in each window as you sing the last part of "Tideo." How many sounds does the new rhythm have?

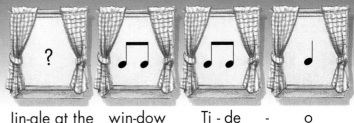

Jin-gle at the   win-dow   Ti - de   -   o

## A "Tideo" Play-Party!

Form two circles, and get ready to **sing** and **move** to "Tideo."

# That Rhythm Again

**Pat** the steady beat as you listen to this song about Johnny's haircut. Then **tap** the rhythm of the words.

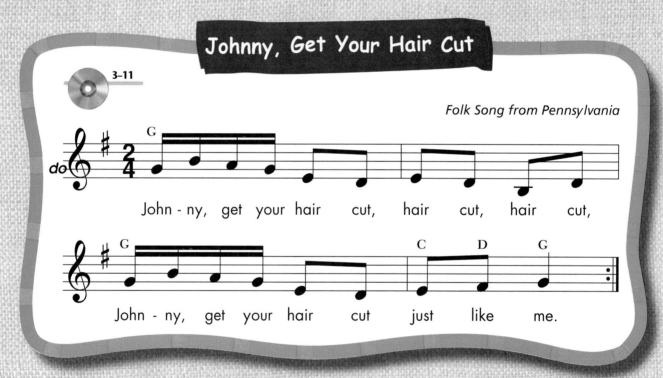

**Johnny, Get Your Hair Cut**

3–11

*Folk Song from Pennsylvania*

John - ny, get your hair   cut,   hair   cut,   hair   cut,

John - ny, get your hair   cut   just   like   me.

## Sing the New Rhythm

This song begins with the new rhythm ♪♪♪♪.
The new rhythm has four sounds and lasts one beat. Find the new rhythm in the song. Then **sing** the song with rhythm syllables.

# Say That Rhythm

Here's a rhyme that also has the new rhythm.
Say the rhyme as you **clap** a steady beat.
Which word does not have the new rhythm?

### Jelly in a Dish

3-12

*Traditional Jump-Rope Rhyme*

Jel - ly   in   a   dish,   Jel - ly   in   a   dish,

Wig - gle   wag - gle,   wig - gle   wag - gle,   Jel - ly   in   a   dish!

# Groups of Two Beats

The rhythm of "Jelly in a Dish" moves in groups of two beats. Each group of two beats forms a **measure.** Measures are separated by **bar lines.**

A **bar line** is a vertical line drawn through a staff to separate measures.

A **measure** is a grouping of beats separated by bar lines.

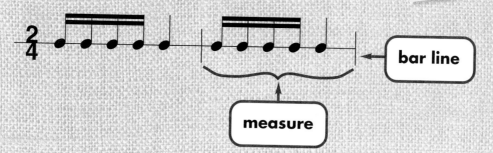

bar line

measure

How many measures are in "Jelly in a Dish"?

## Hear That Rhythm

**Listen** to this selection from a symphony by Franz Joseph Haydn. Count how many times you hear .

3-14
### Symphony in G, No. 88

**Movement 4**
**by Franz Joseph Haydn**
This symphony was composed in 1787, more than 200 years ago.

M·U·S·I·C  M·A·K·E·R·S

# Franz Joseph Haydn

**Franz Joseph Haydn** (1732–1809) composed more than 104 symphonies, more than any other composer! He was born in Austria and he was one of twelve children. When he was eight years old, he was sent to Vienna to be a choirboy. There he continued his musical training.

## Show What You Know!

Here are three rhythm patterns from the beginnings of songs you know. **Clap** and say each rhythm. Name the songs.

1.

2.

3.

**CD-ROM** Create your own rhythm pattern using  with music notation software.

# Takes TWO to CRAWFISH

Boogie like a crawfish as you **listen** to this Cajun dance song. **Move** your arms back and forth as you take sliding steps backward.

3–15

## Crawfish!

*Words and Music by Papillion*

**VERSE**

1. Now there's a funny little dance the Cajun people love to do,
   That when you hear me talk about, you're gonna want to do it too.
   First you shake your little tail, shimmy back a step or two.
   Then put your hands in the air, do like the crawfish do.
   *Refrain*

2. (Instrumental Verse)
   *Refrain*

Craw-fish! Got to do a lit-tle mud bug boo-gie,

Craw-fish! do the mud bug jit-ter-bug boo-gie, Craw-fish!

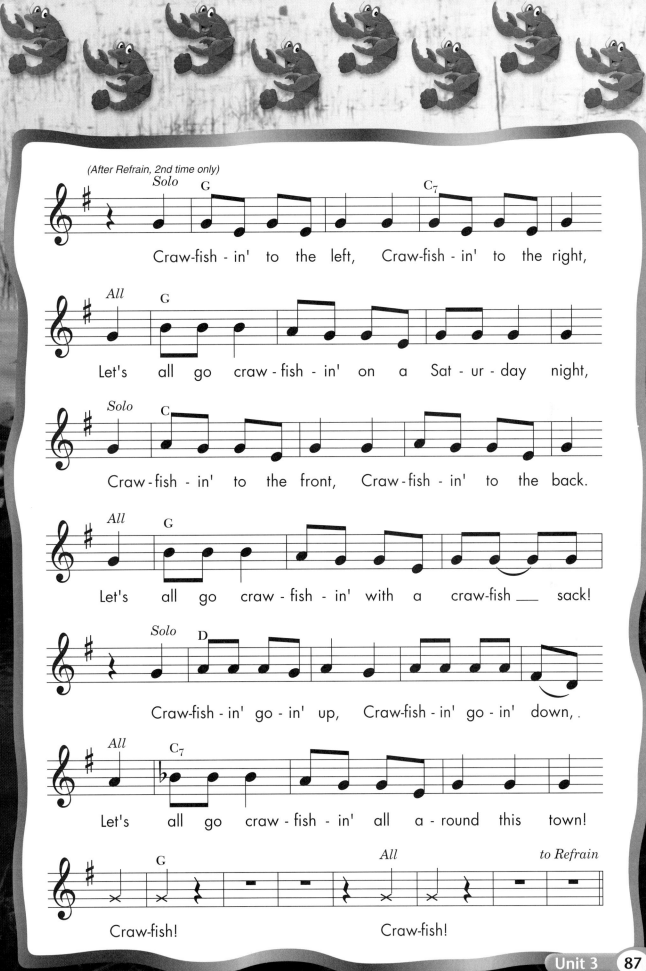

## Do the Mud Bug Boogie

**Sing** "Crawfish!" and **move** with your partner. Count in your head as you **move**, 1-2, 1-2, 1-2.

**Tune In**

Some Cajun people fish for crawfish. They fish in a place called a bayou. A bayou is a swampy creek.

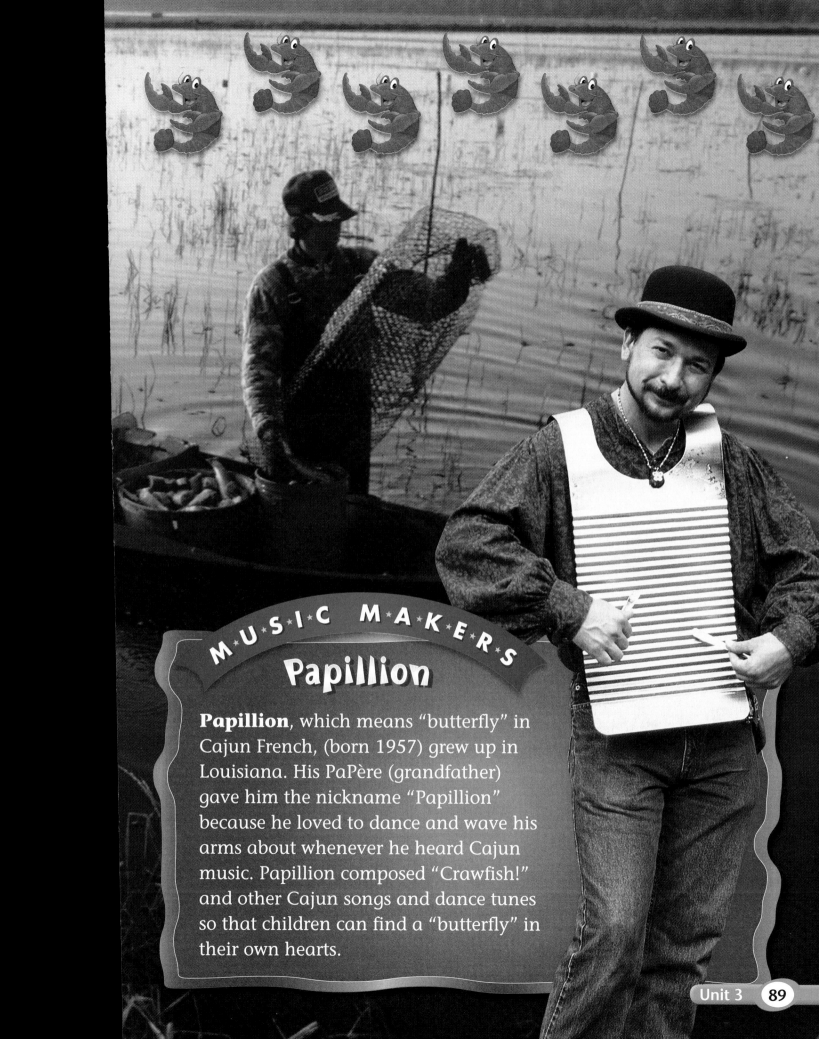

# MUSIC MAKERS

## Papillion

**Papillion**, which means "butterfly" in Cajun French, (born 1957) grew up in Louisiana. His PaPère (grandfather) gave him the nickname "Papillion" because he loved to dance and wave his arms about whenever he heard Cajun music. Papillion composed "Crawfish!" and other Cajun songs and dance tunes so that children can find a "butterfly" in their own hearts.

# What's the **F O R M**?

**Sing** this old folk song from Germany.
Find the **a** and **b** parts in the song.

 3–17

## Ein Männlein steht im Walde
### (A Little Man in the Woods)

*German Words by Hoffmann Von Fallersleben*
*English Words by Bryan Louiselle*

*Folk Song from Germany*

Ein Männ-lein steht im Wal - de ganz still und stumm;
A lit - tle fel - low stands in the woods a - head.

es hat von lau - ter Pur - pur ein Mänt - lein um.
He wears a pur - ple coat with a hint of red.

Sagt, wer mag das Männ-lein sein, das da steht im Wald al - lein
Tell me who this man can be, stand-ing there so pa - tient - ly,

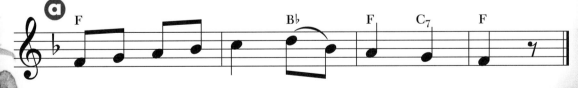

mit dem pur - pur - ro - ten ___ Män - te - lein?
Stand-ing all a - lone in the woods a - head?

## Name Your Pattern

Which pattern below matches the form of the song?

1. **a b a b**   2. **a a b b**   3. **a a b a**

## Into the Woods

*"Ein Männlein steht im Walde"* is also part of the opera *Hänsel und Gretel*. **Listen** to the song as it is sung in the opera. What is the form of the song?

**3-21**

### Ein Männlein steht im Walde

**from *Hänsel und Gretel*
by Engelbert Humperdinck**

In the opera, Gretel sings this folk song when she and Hänsel go to the forest to pick berries.

▲ Hänsel and Gretel from the opera

# Water Melodies

A spring is flowing water that comes up out of the ground. **Listen** to how the melody of this song moves like a spring.

3–22

## Allá en la fuente

### (There at the Spring)

*English Words by Luis Eliezar*

*Folk Song from Mexico*

A - llá en la fuen - te ha - bía un cho - rri - to;
A lit - tle spring, feel - ing ver - y fick - le,

se ha - cía gran - do - te, se ha - cía chi - qui - to;
be - gan a flood, then be - came a trick - le.

es - ta - ba de mal hu - mor, po - bre cho - rri - to te - nía ca - lor.
Too much, and then not e-nough poor lit - tle spring must be in a huff.

▼ Chicago, Illinois

Las Colinas, Texas ▲

# Fountain Music

A spring is like a natural fountain. Many cities and villages around the world have fountains. Sometimes fountains inspire composers to write music.

**Listen** to this music by Respighi [ruh-SPEE-gee]. Use scarves and **move** to show how the music sounds like fountains.

▲ Paris, France

**3–26**

## La fontana di Trevi al meriggio

**from *Fontane di Roma* (Fountains of Rome)**
**by Ottorino Respighi**

Respighi composed this music to celebrate the beauty of the Trevi Fountain in Rome, Italy.

▼ Trevi Fountain, Rome, Italy

# Two Singing Games

"Bow Wow Wow" is a traditional singing game.
As you **sing**, be sure to keep a steady tempo.

3–27

## Bow Wow Wow

*Traditional Singing Game*

Bow wow wow! Whose dog art thou?

Lit - tle Tom - my Tuck - er's dog, Bow wow wow!

*Whose dog art thou?*      *Bow wow wow!*

94

# A Latin American Singing Game

Now **sing** this Latin American game song.
**Compare** the pitches in the color
boxes of both songs. How are they alike?

 3–28

## Naranja dulce
### (Sweet Orange)

*English Words by Eva Laurinda*

*Latin American Singing Game*
*(Mexico and Costa Rica)*

1. Na - ran - ja dul - ce, li - món par - ti - do,
1. Sweet hon - ey or - ange, a slice of le - mon,

da - me un a - bra - zo que yo te pi - do.
give me a hug now, my friend I'll miss you.

2. Si fueran falsos mis juramentos,
en otros tiempos se olvidaran.

3. Toca la marcha, mi pecho llora,
adiós señora, yo ya me voy.

2. It's time to shake hands, true friends are faithful,
I'll not forget you, I wish you well.

3. The march is playing, it's time to go now,
Goodbye my dear friend, I'm sad to leave you.

## Tune In

Children all over the world like to play singing games. "Miss Mary Mack," a hand-clapping game, and "Tideo," a play-party, are popular singing games from the United States.

# Read a NEW PITCH

**Listen** for the new pitch in this folk song.

3–32

## Rocky Mountain

*Folk Song from the Southern United States*

**VERSE**

1. Rock - y moun-tain, rock - y moun-tain, rock - y moun-tain high;

When you're on that rock - y moun-tain, hang your head and cry!

**REFRAIN**

Do, do, do, do, Do re - mem - ber me;

Do, do, do, do, Do re - mem - ber me.

2. Sunny valley, sunny valley,
    sunny valley low;
    When you're in that sunny valley,
    Sing it soft and slow. *Refrain*

3. Stormy ocean, stormy ocean,
    stormy ocean wide;
    When you're on that deep blue sea,
    There's no place you can hide. *Refrain*

## Name the Pitch

The new pitch is between *mi* and *do*.
It is called *re*.

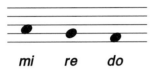

mi    re    do

The hand sign for
*re* looks like this. ▶

## Singing with *re*

Now **sing** "Rocky Mountain." When you get to
the refrain, use hand signs and pitch syllables.

### Tune In

"Rocky Mountain" is from the
southern United States. One of the main
mountain ranges in this area is the Blue
Ridge Mountains, pictured here.

# Chase a Melody

Have you ever seen a squirrel scurry up a tree? **Sing** and show hand signs for "Let Us Chase the Squirrel." Get ready to scurry, too, so you can catch the melody!

3-33

## Let Us Chase the Squirrel

*Folk Song from North Carolina*

1. Let us chase the squir - rel,
2. If you want to catch me,

Up the hick - 'ry, down the hick - 'ry,
Up the hick - 'ry, down the hick - 'ry,

Let us chase the squir - rel,
If you want to catch me,

Up the hick - 'ry tree.
Learn to climb a tree.

# New Places for Pitches

In the song "Let Us Chase the Squirrel," *do* is in the first space on the staff. Look at the first line of the music below. Where is *do* now? Where is *re*?

This time *do* should be on a line, but there are not enough lines on the staff. You can add an extra line for *do* called a **ledger line.**

> A **ledger line** is an extra line used for pitches above or below the staff.

ledger line

## Show What You Know!

Each melody below comes from a song you know that has *re* in it. Find *do* in each example. Then **sing** each melody with pitch syllables and name the tune.

# Colorful

**Listen** to this song. It is from Nigeria, a country in Africa. **Describe** the timbres of the **percussion** instruments that you hear.

**Percussion** instruments are played by shaking, scraping, or striking.

3–34

## Ise oluwa

*Yoruba Folk Song from Nigeria*

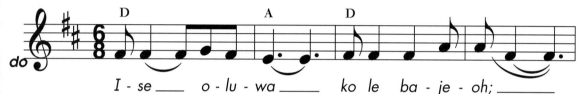

I - se ___ o - lu - wa ___ ko le ba - je - oh; ___

I - se ___ o - lu - wa ___ ko le ba - je - oh. ___

Ko le ba - je - oh, ___ ko le ba - je - oh. ___

I - se ___ o - lu - wa ___ ko le ba - je - oh; ___

I - se ___ o - lu - wa ___ ko le ba - je - oh. ___

# Sounds

## Be an African Drummer!

**Play** these patterns with
"*Ise oluwa.*"

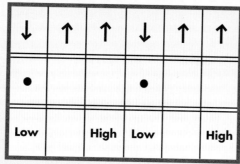

| ↓ | ↑ | ↑ | ↓ | ↑ | ↑ |
|---|---|---|---|---|---|
| • | | | • | | |
| Low | | High | Low | | High |

**Listen** to the marimbas on the recording. They are percussion instruments from Zimbabwe.
**Describe** the timbre.

3–37
### Yuwi maiwe

**Contemporary from Zimbabwe
as performed by Dumisani Maraire**

The marimbas on this recording were handmade by Dumisani Maraire and his students.

# Percussion from Bali

The *gamelan* is a set of instruments from Bali. It includes percussion. **Listen** to this recording to learn how the *kendang*, the *gong*, the *gangsa*, and the *kempli* sound.

3–38

**Gamelan Instruments Montage**

▲ *Gamelan*

How many percussion instruments do you see? What are they made of?

 **Video Library** Watch *Percussion Instruments: Tuned* to see and hear an example of *gamelan*.

## Gamelan Game

**Listen** to the way instruments weave their sounds together in *Ujan mas*. Point to the instruments as you hear them in the recording.

3–39

**by Gde Purana**

*Ujan mas* means "golden rain" in Balinese.

# Ujan mas Listening Map

**Gong**

**Gangsa**

**Kendang**

**Kempli**

# Creating Textures

What do you do while waiting for a traffic light to change? You can **sing** this song as you wait.

**Play** these ostinatos with the song to create a thicker texture.

Alto Metallophone

Bass Xylophone

# Waiting for the Traffic Light

*Words and Music by David Connors*

**Swing Style**

We're wait-ing for the traf-fic light to turn to green.

If it ev-er hap-pens it re-mains to be seen. As we

wait for the light we will start to move.

We can feel the rhy-thm and get in-to the groove.

Move to the right. Move to the left.

Move in a way that you like best.

Ev-'ry-one back, turn 'round and 'round,

Ev-'ry-one for-ward, touch the ground.

# Playing Lullaby Layers

**Sing** this lullaby from Africa. Abiyoyo is a character in South African folk stories.

3–42

## ABIYOYO

*Bantu Lullaby*

A - bi - yo - yo, _____ a - bi - yo - yo, _____

A - bi - yo - yo, _____ a - bi - yo - yo; _____

A - bi - yo - yo, bi - yo - yo, bi - yo - yo, _____

A - bi - yo - yo, bi - yo - yo, bi - yo - yo. _____

## Building Music Layers

**Play** these patterns with the song. Each pattern adds a new layer of sound.

**Describe** how adding the layers changes the texture of the music. Does the texture become thinner or thicker?

▼ Many African lullabies are about scary monsters like Abiyoyo.

# Putting It

## What Do You Know?

**1.** Look at the rhythm of "Tideo" on page 80. Find and point to the following rhythms.

**a.** ♫    **b.** ♩.    **c.** ♫♫♫

**2.** Look at "Tideo" again.

  **a.** Find and point to the barlines.
  **b.** How many measures are in the song?

**3.** Read the pitches in "Bow Wow Wow" on page 94. How many times does each of these pitches occur in the song?

  **a.** *so*     **b.** *la*     **c.** *mi*     **d.** *re*     **e.** *do*

## What Do You Hear? 3

Listen to the four rhythm patterns on the recording. Match the patterns you hear with the rhythms below.

**a.**

**b.**

**c.** 

**d.**

# All Together

## Move with an Accent

Move to show the accented and unaccented beats in "Crawfish!" Perform larger movements for accented beats. Perform smaller movements for unaccented beats.

## Perform Rhythms

As you listen to the recording of "Tideo," pat each of these rhythm patterns.

a.

b.

## Create a Melody

Create a melody for "Jelly in a Dish." Use only these pitches.

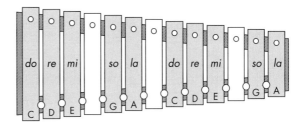

do re mi so la do re mi so la
C D E G A C D E G A

Have your melody end on *do*. Perform your melody on a xylophone or metallophone.

## Samba!

In the 1930s, Carmen Miranda came to the United States from Brazil. She brought with her the *samba* style of music. **Listen** to *Chica chica boom chic* and **move** to the music.

**4–5**

### Chica chica boom chic

**by Mack Gordon and Harry Warren**

In this song, Miranda expresses her pride in being Brazilian.

Here is a *samba* rhythm you can **play** along with the recording.

## M·U·S·I·C  M·A·K·E·R·S

### Carmen Miranda

**Carmen Miranda** (1909–1955) was famous as the Banana Lady. She appeared in TV commercials and advertisements for bananas. She was known for her "tutti-frutti" hat. Miranda became a singing, dancing movie star in Hollywood.

# Building Our Musical Skills

# Going Bananas

Here is a song about bananas you can **sing**.

**4–6**

# Banana

*Words and Music by Flor De Caña*

**REFRAIN**
*All*

All    the na-tions like ba-na-na. _____

All    the rac-es like ba-na-na. __

# Expressing the

How do storms make you feel? How does the child in the song feel about this tropical storm?

**Listen** to *"La tormenta tropical."* When the song gets gradually louder, this is called a **crescendo.** Find the *crescendos* in the music.

> A **crescendo** is a word or music symbol tells the performer to get gradually louder.

 4–8

# La tormenta tropical

## (The Tropical Storm)

*Words and Music by Juanita Newland Ulloa*

**VERSE**

1. *Despierta, hija, despierta,*
   *es hora de levantar.*
   *No importa si hay sol o lluvia,*
   *es hora de estudiar.*
   Refrain

2. *Entonces cierro las ventanas*
   *el viento soplará.*
   *El cielo estara enojado*
   *y pronto llorará.*
   Refrain

3. *Por fin sale el sol.*
   *El viento se calló.*
   *las gotas se apagan*
   *la lluvia se paró.*
   Refrain

1. Wake up, wake up, oh my dear one.
   Wake up and start a new day.
   No matter if there's sun or raindrops,
   We've much to do on this day.
   *Refrain*

2. We'll stay inside while it's raining.
   Let's get the windows shut tight.
   The sky is getting dark like it's nighttime!
   Sit here with me 'til it's light.
   *Refrain*

3. We'll listen to the storm raging.
   Glad we're inside on this day.
   Tomorrow we'll go out and see puddles,
   When the dark clouds all go away.
   *Refrain*

# Weather

**REFRAIN** *f*

Ay   ma - mi, no quier-o des-per-tar - me.
Oh,   please, mom-my,  I  don't want to  wake   up.

*p*

Al - go  pa - sa,  lo ____ sien - to   ya. ____
I   can  see   that  storm _ clouds are  here. _

*f*

Es  que  vie - ne,  vie - ne  la  tor - men - ta,
I   can  feel   that  some - thing is ____ com - ing.

la  tor - men - ta  trop - i - cal. ____
Now the  tropi - cal   storm _  is   near. ____

## A Weather Proverb

A proverb is a wise old saying.
Say this proverb about weather.

"Whether it's cold or whether it's hot,
We shall have weather, whether or not."

Decide which words to say loudly or softly.
Which words might get accents? Where can
you make a *crescendo*?

## Creating with Expression

- **Compose** a melody for the proverb using
only these pitches.

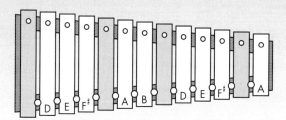

- Teach your melody to a partner.

- **Perform** your melody with dynamics.

# Listening for Expression

**Listen** to *Saudação*. How does the listening map show changes in the dynamics? What parts of the map show loud or soft?

4–12
## Saudação

**from *Concerto for Marimba and String Orchestra***
**by Ney Rosauro**

Rosauro is a composer from Brazil. He writes music for marimba and other percussion.

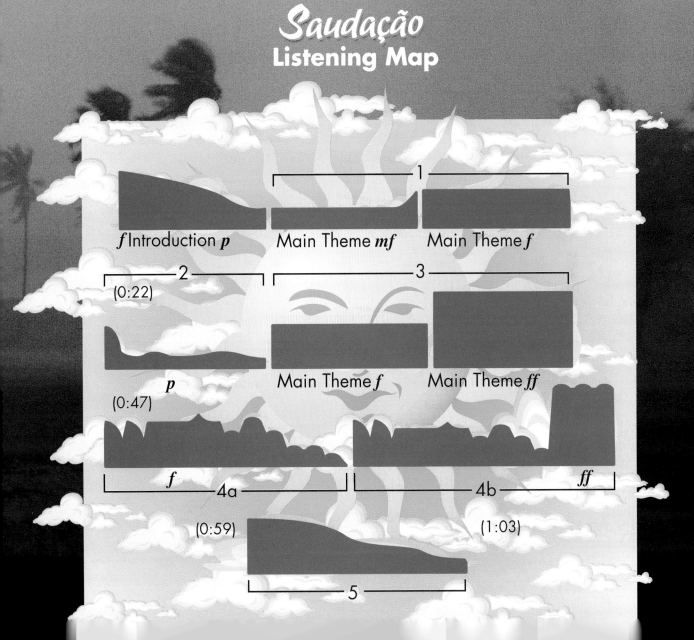

*Saudação*
### Listening Map

**1**

*f* Introduction *p*      Main Theme *mf*      Main Theme *f*

**2**
(0:22)

*p*
(0:47)

**3**

Main Theme *f*      Main Theme *ff*

*f*      4a      4b      *ff*

(0:59)      (1:03)

5

# Banjo Rhythms

What instument does Dinah play in the song?
Now **sing** "Dinah."

4–13

## Dinah

*Folk Song from the United States*

No one's in the house but Di - nah, Di - nah,

No one's in the house but me, I know.

No one's in the house but Di - nah, Di - nah,

Strum - min' on the old ban - jo.

## Sing Your Name

**Sing** the song again. Sing your name and
the name of an instrument you'd like to play!

# Dinah's Got Rhythm!

The rhythms in each house equal one beat.
**Listen** to "Dinah" again. Can you find each
rhythm in the song?

# You've Got Rhythm!

**Clap** and say the rhythm in each house. Then
put the houses in any order to **compose** your
own rhythm piece. **Perform** it on an instrument.

*Arts* **Connection**

◄ *The Banjo Lesson*
by Mary Cassatt
(1844–1926)

**Element: RHYTHM** | **Skill: CREATING** | **Connection: SOCIAL STUDIES**

# Cooking with Rhythm

**Sing** this song and **move** the way the words tell you!

## Old Brass Wagon

4–15

*Play-Party from the United States*

1. Cir - cle to the left, old brass wag - on;
2. Cir - cle to the right, old brass wag - on;

Cir - cle to the left, old brass wag - on;
Cir - cle to the right, old brass wag - on;

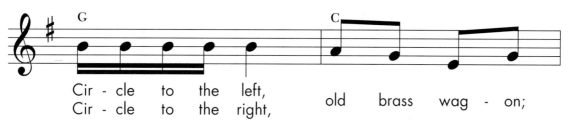

Cir - cle to the left, old brass wag - on;
Cir - cle to the right, old brass wag - on;

You're the one, my dar - lin'.

3. Swing, oh, swing, . . .
4. Promenade right, . . .

5. Walk it up and down, . . .
6. Break and swing, . . .

## Rhythm Stew

Look for this rhythm pattern
in "Old Brass Wagon."

How many times did
you find it?

**Create** a rhythm piece with
these rhythms.

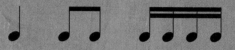

**Play** your piece on fun
instruments. Maybe try spoons!

## Show What You Know!

These rhythm patterns are from songs you know. What
words go with them? Name and **sing** the songs they
came from.

1. $\frac{2}{4}$

2. $\frac{2}{4}$

# A Longer Sound

**Listen** to "*Frère Jacques*." **Tap** the steady beat. Which sounds last for more than one beat? Find them on this chart.

dor - mez    vous? →

din    dan    don →

# One + One = ?

Some sounds in *"Frère Jacques"* last more than one beat.

♩ = 1 beat

♩ + ♩ = 2 beats

You can use a **tie** to join the two notes together.

♩ ♩ = 2 beats

tie

A **tie** is a musical symbol that joins two notes together to create a longer sound.

Find the ties in the music.
Then **sing** the song in French and English.

4–20

## Frère Jacques

### (Are You Sleeping?)

*Folk Song from France*

Frè - re    Jac - ques,    Frè - re    Jac - ques,
Are    you    sleep - ing,    Are    you    sleep - ing,

Dor - mez    vous? ____    Dor - mez    vous? ____
Broth - er    John, ____    Broth - er    John? ____

Son - nez les ma - ti - nes,    Son - nez les ma - ti - nes,
Morn-ing bells are ring - ing,    Morn-ing bells are ring - ing,

Din,    dan,    don, ____    din,    dan,    don. ____
Ding,    dang,    dong, ____    ding,    dang,    dong. ____

# Phrases That Move You!

A **phrase** is a part of a melody.
The melody of this song has four phrases.
**Listen** to hear where each phrase ends.

A **phrase** is a musical sentence.

4–24  A Song That's Just for You

*Words and Music by Bryan Louiselle*

It may be high or low, It may be fast or slow,

It may be short or long. ___

It could be rap or rock, It could be bop or Bach,

It could be soft or strong. _

124

## Play Phrase Statues

Play a statue game with your classmates.
Stand in a circle. At the end of each phrase,
jump into the center and pose like a statue.

It does-n't mat-ter what the tune ___ is,

or if the style is old ___ or new; ___

If you en-joy the sound, it means you might have found _

a song that's just for you. ___

# Miles of Melody

Long ago, English children sang this song. They pretended they could travel all the way to Babylon in just one day. **Sing** the song and **play** the game.

4–26

## How Many Miles to Babylon?

*Game Song from England*

do

How ma-ny miles to Ba - by - lon? Three score and ten.

Will we be there by can - dle - light? Yes, and back a - gain.

O - pen the gates and let us through. Not with-out a beck and bow.

Here's your beck; here's your bow! O-pen the gates and let us through.

# Miles to Go for *mi re do!*

Find the places in the song with *mi*, *re*, and *do* only. **Sing** those places with pitch syllables.

"Here's your beck"

"Here's your bow"

"Open the gates and let us through"

**Tune In**

Babylon was once a city near present-day Baghdad, Iraq.

Grow a Melody

The melody for this song was written by children from Upper Nyack, New York. The words are from a proverb, or wise old saying.

 4–30

## Plant Four Seeds

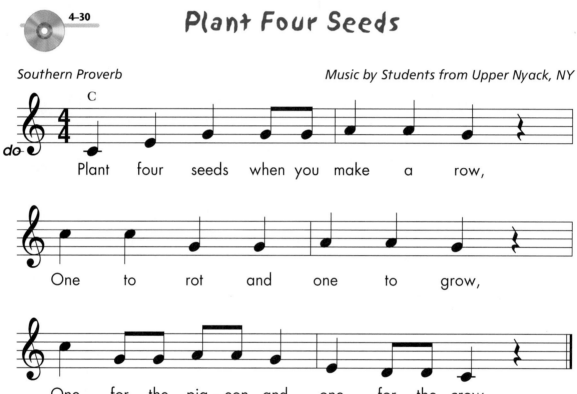

*Southern Proverb*                    *Music by Students from Upper Nyack, NY*

Plant four seeds when you make a row,

One to rot and one to grow,

One for the pig - eon and one for the crow.

**Play** these patterns with the song.

Bass Xylophone

Xylophone

Squash

Tomatoes

Daffodils

Rutabagas

# Create a Sound Garden

**Compose** a melody to add a new section to "Plant Four Seeds." Use names of flowers and vegetables you might plant in your garden. Here is an example.

Xylophone

Ru - ta - ba - ga, squash,     ros - es,   dai - sy.

Use only these pitches in your melody.

# A Melody Without Words

**Listen** to the way this composer created a melody with these pitches.

4–32
**Allegretto**

**by Gunild Keetman**
On this recording you will hear xylophones, maracas, tambourine, and tom-toms.

# A Flood of Sound

**Listen** for the ♫ rhythm in this speech piece.
When you hear it, shuffle your feet in that rhythm.

4-33

## Mississippi River Chant

*by Bill Martin Jr.*

Mississippi River morning Mississippi **sun,**
Mississippi River warning thunder wonder **done.**
Mississippi River raining Mississippi **flood,**
Mississippi River waning oozy newsy **mud.**
Shuffle to the **left** shuffle to the **left,**
shuffle shuffle shuffle shuffle,
shuffle to the **left.**
Mississippi River morning Mississippi **sun,**
Mississippi River warning thunder wonder **done.**

# Mississippi Melody

**Play** rhythms from the speech piece on a xylophone. Use only these pitches.

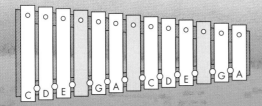

# Mississippi Rhythm

Now **compose** an ostinato with words from the speech piece. **Play** it on one of these instruments.

# A Five-Pitch Song

In Korea a bell rings to start the school day. How does your school day begin? **Listen** to this Korean school song. Which words sound like a bell?

# Five Familiar Pitches

*"Ha'kyo jung"* has five pitches that you already know. **Listen** to the song again. What pitch ends the song? Hint: The song starts on *so*.

# Ha'kyo jung
## (School Bell Sounding)

*English Words by David Eddleman*

*School Song from Korea*
*Words and Music by Mary Kimm Joh*

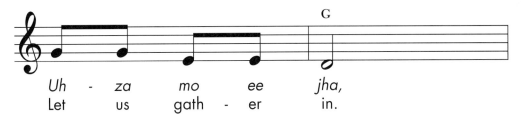

1. Ha' - kyo jung ee daeng daeng daeng,
1. School bell sound - ing, ding, dong, ding,

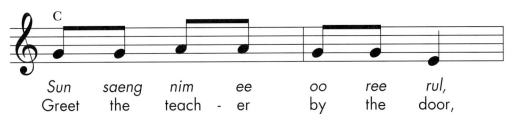

Uh - za mo ee jha,
Let us gath - er in.

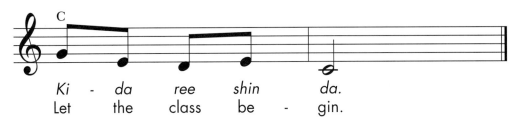

Sun saeng nim ee oo ree rul,
Greet the teach - er by the door,

Ki - da ree shin da.
Let the class be - gin.

2. Ha'kyo jung ee daeng daeng daeng,
   Uhza mo ee jha,
   Sa ee joht keh oh nuhldoh,
   Khong bu jhal ha jha.

2. School bell sounding, ding, dong, ding,
   Let us gather in.
   Working all together now,
   Learning once again.

## Sing a Pentatonic Song

When a song ends on *do* and has only four other pitches, it is called *do* **pentatonic.** Now **sing** *"Ha'kyo jung"* with pitch syllables and hand signs.

## Play Along with the Song

Here are some patterns you can **play** as the class sings *"Ha'kyo jung."*

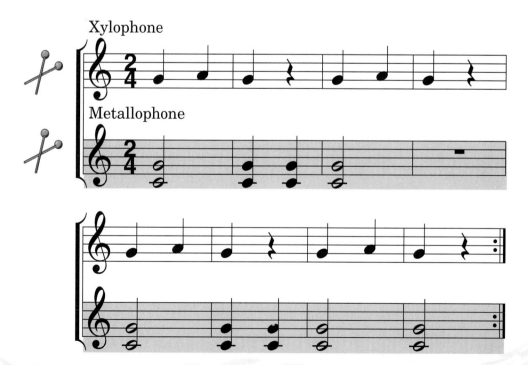

# Hearing Pentatonic

**Listen** to *Arirang,* one of the most well-known folk songs from Korea. Each section ends on *do.* Raise your hand when you hear *do* in the recording.

4–39
## Arirang
**Traditional from Korea**
**as performed by the Dieter Ilg Trio**
This traditional melody is performed here by a jazz group.

## Show What You Know!

Each of these melodies comes from a song you may know. **Sing** each one with pitch syllables and hand signs.

1. do   mi   so   la   mi mi re re do

2. do do re re mi   so   do do re re do

3. do do mi so do   mi   do do mi so re

# String Sounds

Some string instruments are played with a bow. Some are plucked, and some are struck like percussion.

**Listen** to these string players perform a lively dance tune. **Describe** the different timbres you hear.

## Tune In

String instruments make sound because their strings vibrate.

▼ hammered dulcimer

▼ string bass

## More String Sounds

See and hear more examples of string instruments by going to the Sound Bank on page 392. Find the viola, cello, banjo, guitar, and the mountain dulcimer. How are they the same or different from the instruments in *Cold and Frosty Morning?*

4–40

### Cold and Frosty Morning

**Traditional English Country Dance Tune**

Some of the instruments on this recording are Celtic harp, string bass, hammered dulcimer, and fiddle.

▼ Celtic harp

fiddle
(violin) ▶

# Electric Strings

Some string players change the way their instruments sound by attaching an electronic "pickup." The "pickup" sends the sound to other electronic equipment which changes the sound.

▼ pickup

▼ amplifier

▲ "wah" pedal

## An Electric Fiddle

**Listen** to Eileen Ivers play her electric blue fiddle. *Fiddle* is another name for the violin. Notice when the fiddle sounds "normal" and when it sounds very different. **Describe** what you hear.

4-41
### Riverdance Suite
**by John Whelan**

This piece is an arrangement of some of the music from the dance show *Riverdance*.

## MUSIC MAKERS

### Eileen Ivers

**Eileen Ivers** (born 1965) is one of the top fiddle players in the world today. She was born in New York City and spent much of her childhood in both New York and Ireland. Ivers won her first award for fiddle playing when she was nine years old. She is most famous for playing fiddle in the show *Riverdance*.

# Turkish Textures

**Sing** this folk song from Turkey, a country in the Middle East.

 5–1

## *Adana ya gidelim*
### (Let's Go to Adana)

*English Words by C. P. Language Institute*                    *Folk Song from Turkey*

A - da - na ____ ya ____ gi - de - lim.
Let's    go    to    A - da - na    and    eat    or - an - ges.

Por - ta - kal - lar - i ____ yi - ye - lim.
There _ they _ have    the    sweet - est ____ or - an - ges.

**Play** this pattern with the song. It will sound good as an **accompaniment.**

An **accompaniment** is music that is performed with a melody.

Xylophone

# Texture Time!

Say and **play** the words *Let's go to Adana* on a hand drum.

Let's go to A - da - na.

**Create** a thicker texture by playing this ostinato on a wood block.

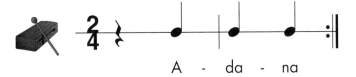

A - da - na

**Play** finger cymbals to give a little "zing" to the texture.

**Video Library** Describe the texture of the music you hear in *Performing in Groups.*

Element: **TEXTURE/HARMONY** | Skill: **PLAYING** | Connection: **RELATED ARTS**

# Music Among

A long time ago, stars helped
sailors find their way around the oceans.

**Sing** this starry song.

5–7

## Oh, Watch the Stars

*Folk Song from South Carolina*

Oh,    watch the    stars,    see how they run.

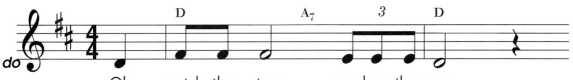

Oh,    watch the    stars,    see how they run. _____

The _ stars run   down _____ at the set-ting of the sun.

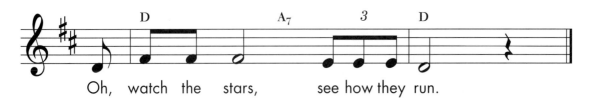

Oh,    watch    the    stars,    see how they    run.

# the Stars

## Playing Among the Stars

Now **play** this ostinato with the song. Which hand moves right and left?

Alto metallophone

**Compose** other "twinkly" sounds to add to your starry texture.

*Arts* **Connection**

◀ *Starry Night, 1923–1924* by Edvard Munch

# Putting It

## What Do You Know?

Read the melodies below. Then find and point to all the pitches called *re*. How many did you find in each?

a.

b.

**5–9**

## What Do You Hear? 4A

You will hear three musical examples. Each example has two phrases. Decide if the phrases in each example are the same or different.

**1.** same          different
**2.** same          different
**3.** same          different

**5–12**

## What Do You Hear? 4B

Listen to these string instruments. Decide how each is being played.

**1.** bowed      plucked      struck
**2.** bowed      plucked      struck
**3.** bowed      plucked      struck

# All Together

## Perform Rhythms

Pat each of these rhythm patterns. Then say the rhythms, using syllables.

a.

b.

c.

## Create a Melody

Choose two of the patterns above and create a pentatonic melody.

• Decide which pattern will be first.

• Use the pitches *do, re, mi, so,* and *la.*

• End your melody on *do.*

• Sing your melody, using the pitch syllables.

## Ways to Explore

If you could not see, how would you learn about the world? Close your eyes and learn through your ears and hands.

**Sing** this song that expresses how much you can learn through touch.

5–15

# I See with My Hands

*Words and Music by Marcy Marxer*

**VERSE**

1. I see with _ my hands    The clouds, the sky, the land;

The fish that swim in the deep blue sea,

The sun that shines on you and me.    I see with _ my hands.

**REFRAIN**

See, _____    see, _____

ev - 'ry cur - i - os - i - ty; _____

### Discovering New Musical Horizons

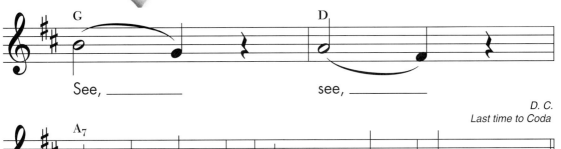

See, _____ see, _____

*D. C.*
*Last time to Coda*

in my hands I hold the key. _____

*Coda (after verse 3 only)*

*(Repeat 2 times)*

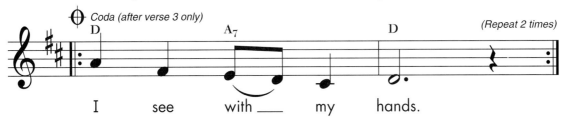

I see with ___ my hands.

2. I see with my hands
   The clouds, the sky, the land;
   A bird, a flow'r, a warm embrace,
   And my best friend's smiling face.
   I see with my hands. *Refrain*

3. I see with my hands
   The clouds, the sky, the land;
   A stone, a stream, a melody,
   The people in my family.
   I see with my hands. *Refrain*

## Listening to Learn

Follow the map as you **listen** to *Fanfarre*.
**Compare** the dynamics of the guitars with the
other instruments. How are they different?

**5–17**

### Fanfarre (Allegro Marziale)

**from *Concierto Madrigal for Two Guitars and Orchestra*
by Joaquín Rodrigo**

Rodrigo composed this piece especially for the guitarists
perfoming on this recording, the Romeros.

## Fanfarre Listening Map

# MUSIC MAKERS

## Joaquín Rodrigo

**Joaquín Rodrigo** (1901–1999), born in Spain, was blind from age three due to illness. He started studying music at a young age and won many awards for his compositions. He was one of Spain's leading composers of the twentieth century.

# Connected Sounds— Separated Sounds

A melody can sound smooth and connected. It can also sound short and separated. **Listen** to "Party Tonight!" **Identify** the parts that are *legato* and the parts that are *staccato*.

A *legato* melody has smooth, connected pitches.

A *staccato* melody has short, separated pitches.

5–18

## Party Tonight!

*Words and Music by Jill Gallina*

*With a Swing*

All    the    an - i - mals    at    the    zoo __

are    hav - ing    a    par - ty    to - night. __

Hop - pin'    and    bop - pin',    roll - in'    and    rock - in',

did    you    ev - er    see    such    a    sight? __

## Moving *Legato*, Moving *Staccato*

**Move** like the animals. To show *legato*, you can swing your arms and turn around. To show *staccato*, you can use short hops and twists. You can also **create** your own movements.

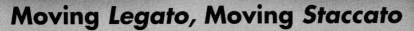

1. Hip-hop-pin' hip - pos,   the grace-ful danc-ing bears,
2. A rock-in' rhin - o,   a waltz-ing pea-cock too,

stomp, stomp-in' el - e - phants _ so loud it hurts our ears. _
swing danc-in' mon-keys and _ a twist-in' kan-ga-roo. _

A hy-e-na does the hu - la,   oh, what a sight!
There's a bal-let danc-ing zeb-ra,

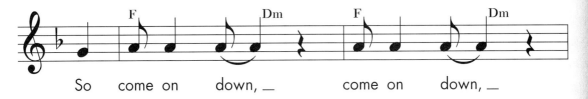

So come on down, _ come on down, _

join our par - ty to - night. __

# Listening for *Legato* and *Staccato*

**Listen** to *Toccata and Tango*. Do the percussion instruments sound *legato* or *staccato*? How do the string instruments sound?

5–20

## Toccata and Tango

**by David Hanson**

The solo percussionist is Steve Houghton. After making this recording he said, ". . . one of life's great pleasures is making music with your friends!"

## M·U·S·I·C M·A·K·E·R·S
### Steve Houghton

**Steve Houghton** (born 1954) is a percussionist, jazz drummer, composer, and teacher. He performs with symphony orchestras and jazz ensembles. He has spent many years teaching percussion to young people.

# A *Legato* and *Staccato* Dance

**Create** a dance to *Toccata and Tango*. Show *staccato* with short, sudden movements. **Move** smoothly with a flowing scarf to show *legato*.

# Two Beats Long

**Listen** to this Spanish song from Costa Rica.
Which sounds are longer than the others?

5–21

## Mariposita
### (Little Butterfly)

English Words by Eva Laurinda

Words and Music by Wilber Alpírez Quesada

Lin - da ma - ri - po - sa    que jue - gas fe - liz, ___
Pret - ty but - ter - fly, ___   play-ing cheer-ful - ly, ___

en - tre tan - tas flo - res,    en - tre tan - tas ro - sas.
in the flow - er gar - den,    with the man - y ros - es.

Prés - ta - me tus a - las,    tus a - las pre - cio - sas,
Let me try your wings, ___   pre-cious lit - tle wings ___ so

que tam - bién yo quie - ro,    ju - gar con las ro - sas.
I can al - so play ___ with    all the pret - ty ros - es.

154

# Singing Long Sounds

Now **sing** "Mariposita." Make sure that you sing  for two whole beats.

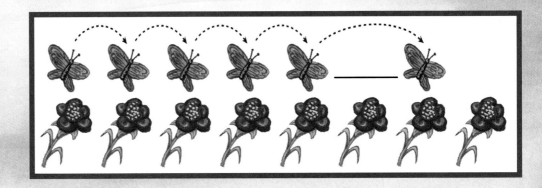

## Two Beat Moves

**Sing** the song again. **Move** to show the difference between the shorter and longer sounds.

**CD-ROM** Use the *Making Music* software to create rhythm patterns with short and long sounds.

# Two Beats in One

In China the melody of "*Hui jia qü*" is played as the children line up to go home from school.

5–25

## *Hui jia qü*

### (Home from School)

English Words by David Eddleman                    Folk Song from China

功　课＿＿　完　毕＿＿　要　回　家
Gong　ke＿＿　wan　bi＿＿　yao　hui　jia
When　the＿＿　sun　is＿＿　sink - ing　low,

收　拾＿＿　书　包　回　家＿＿　去
Shou　shi＿＿　shu　bao　hui　jia＿＿　qü
Home - ward＿　from　my　school　I＿＿＿　go,

看　见＿＿　父　母＿＿　行　个　礼
Kan　jian＿＿　fu　mu＿＿　xing　ge　li
There　where＿　I　know＿　I　will　find

父　母＿＿　对＿＿　我＿＿　笑　嘻　嘻
Fu　mu＿＿　dui＿＿　wo＿＿　xiao　xi　xi.
Wait - ing,＿＿　fa - ther　and　moth - er　kind.

# Read a New Note

**Sing** *"Hui jia qü"* and **tap** the beat. One of the notes lasts for two beats. It can be written like this: ♩ or like this: ♩♩

**Find** each ♩ in the song. **Sing** the song again with rhythm syllables.

**Play** this pattern with the song.

**Arts Connection**

*Jinshan Peasant Painting.* Jinshan is a county in China, near Shanghai. This is a painting of children playing in a schoolyard. ▶

# Elephant Rhythms

Children in Chile sing this game song. Look for each ♩ in *"Un elefante."* **Sing** the song with rhythm syllables.

**5–29**

## Un elefante

**(An Elephant)**

*Singing Game from Chile*
*Words and Music by Claudina de Ferrari*

*English Words by Alice Firgau*

1. Un    e - le - fan - te    se    ba - lan - cea - ba
1. There    on    a    cob - web    made    by    a    spi - der

so - bre    la    te - la    deu - na a - ra - ña,
Sat    a    big    el - e - phant a - swing - ing,

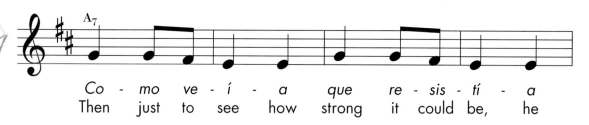

Co - mo    ve - í - a    que    re - sis - tí - a
Then    just    to    see    how    strong    it    could be,    he

fue    a    lla - mar a un    ca - ma - ra - da.
called    for    a    friend    to    come and    join    him.

158

## Add Instruments

**Play** these patterns with *"Un elefante."* Imagine the drum is an elephant. Imagine the finger cymbals are the spider weaving its web.

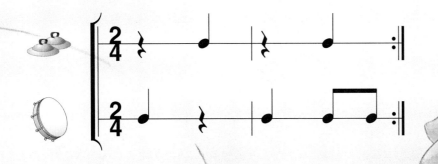

2. *Dos elefantes*
   *se balanceaban*
   *sobre la tela de una araña,*
   *Como veían que resistía*
   *fueron a llamar*
   *a un camarada.*

3. *Tres elefantes . . .*
4. *Cuatro elefantes . . .*
5. *Cinco elefantes . . .*
6. *Seis elefantes . . .*
7. *Siete elefantes . . .*
8. *Ocho elefantes . . .*
9. *Nueve elefantes . . .*
10. *Diez elefantes . . .*

2. There on a cobweb
   made by a spider
   Sat two big elephants a-swinging,
   Then just to see how strong it could be,
   They called for a friend
   to come and join them.

3. . . .Sat three big elephants . . .
4. . . .Sat four big elephants . . .
5. . . .Sat five big elephants . . .
6. . . .Sat six big elephants . . .
7. . . .Sat seven big elephants . . .
8. . . .Sat eight big elephants . . .
9. . . .Sat nine big elephants . . .
10. . . .Sat ten big elephants . . .

## Let's Play an Elephant Game

To play the game, one person pretends to be an elephant balancing on one strand of a spider's web. Can you imagine that? With each new verse, another person joins the game.

Find the rhythm patterns on the spider webs that add up to two beats. How many beats are in the other spider webs?

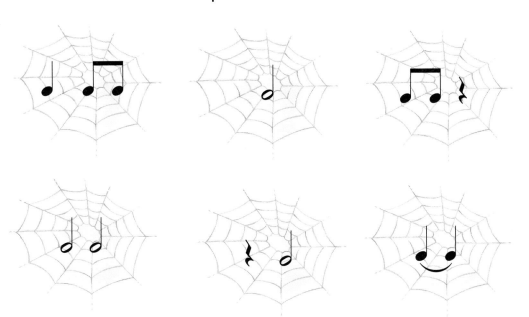

**Tune In**

Some tropical spiders live in groups in large webs. They cooperate to build and repair the web.

| Element: FORM | Skill: SINGING | Connection: CULTURE |

# Questions and Answers

This song is in question and answer form. A musical question is a phrase that seems to need a musical answer. As you **sing** "Same Train," find the question and answer phrases.

 5–33

## Same Train

*English Version by Holsaert-Bailey*                    *African American Folk Melody*

```
    D                          G
1.  Same    train _    a - blow - in'  at    the sta - tion,
2.  Same    train _    a - com - in' down the  line, __
```

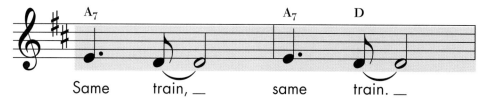

```
    A7                         A7          D
    Same    train, __    same      train. __
```

```
    D
    Same    train _    wait - in' for   the peo - ple,
    Same    train _    pick - in' up ___  speed, __
```

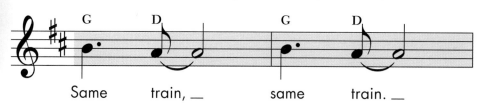

```
    G        D              G        D
    Same    train, __    same      train. __
```

Same train __ leav - in' the sta - tion,
Same train __ go - in' like six - ty,

Same train __ be back to - mor - row,

Same train, __ same train. __

3. Same train a-chuggin' up the mountain, } 2 times
   Hard pull, hard pull,
   Same train easy down the mountain,
   Same train be back tomorrow, . . .

4. Same train a-passin' all the farmyards, } 2 times
   Same train, same train.
   Same train a-passin' all the farmyards,
   Same train be back tomorrow, . . .

5. Same train a-whistlin' at the crossroads, } 2 times
   Same train, same train.
   Same train a-whistlin' at the crossroads,
   Same train be back tomorrow, . . .

6. Same train a-comin' to the tunnel, . . .
   Same train a-speedin' through the tunnel, . . .
   Same train out in the sunlight,
   Same train be back tomorrow, . . .

7. Same train a-blowin' for the station, . . .
   Same train a-stoppin' at the station, . . .
   Same train a-droppin' all the people,
   Same train be back tomorrow, . . .

# Two Sections,

Some songs have more than one section. **Listen** to "Clear the Kitchen." What clues tell you where a new section begins?

 5–34

# Clear the Kitchen

Folk Song from Pennsylvania

**A**  B♭

Down in Vir - gin - ia one af - ter - noon,

B♭  F

We swept the floor with a brand new broom;

B♭  F  B♭

And then we all would form a ring,

B♭  F  B♭

And this is the song that we would sing: ___

# Two Movements

## Kitchen Dance

How would you *clear the kitchen?*

- **Create** movements for the Ⓐ section of the song.
- **Move** a different way for the Ⓑ section.

**B**

F₇

"Clear the kitch - en, young folks, old folks,

B♭

Clear the kitch - en, young folks, old folks.

B♭  F₇  B♭

Old Vir - gin - ia nev - er tires!"

# Dinosaur Forms

**Listen** to "Dinosaur Dance." Does this song have Ⓐ and Ⓑ sections only? There is a new section at the very end of the song with this symbol ⊕. It is called a **coda.**

A **coda** is a short section added to the end of a song.

 6–1

*Words and Music by Ned Ginsburg*

# Dinosaur Dance

### VERSE

1. Thousands and thousands
   of years ago,
   dinosaurs ruled the land.
   They plodded through their
   humdrum lives,
   and snow and mud and sand!
   But ev'ry once in a while,
   even dinosaurs need some fun.
   So they'd throw themselves a party
   right out in the scorching sun!
   And to this day,
   we celebrate the dinosaur way:
   *Refrain*

2. You don't need fancy
   dancin' shoes,
   don't strut your stylish stuff.
   Just do like a
   brontosaurus,
   that's sure to be enough!
   And don't make fun of your neighbor.
   'cause he's liable to chew you out!
   Just join in the jumpin' madness,
   that's what it's all about.
   Now, once again,
   you got to get ready, my friend:
   *Refrain*

Lift your di-no-saur knee, wig-gle your di-no-saur toes,

raise your di-no-saur hand, and touch your di-no-saur nose.

# Dinosaur Dancing

**Create** a dance that shows the difference between the **A** and **B** sections of the song. How will you **move** for the *coda*?

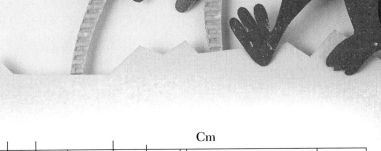

Wag your di-no-saur tail,    now hold your di-no-saur stance.

*D. C. Last time to ⊕*

Whad-da-ya know?   You're do-in' the di - no-saur dance!

⊕ *Coda*

Whad-da - ya know?    You're do - in'  the  di - no - saur

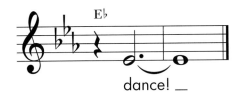

dance! _

**Element: MELODY** | **Skill: SINGING** | **Connection: CULTURE**

# A MELODY to Sing

"All Around the Buttercup" is a singing game. How many phrases are in the song? As you **sing** the song, notice how the phrases end.

## All Around the Buttercup

6–3

*Traditional Singing Game from the United States*

do — All a-round the but-ter cup, one, two, three.

If you want a nice young friend, just choose me.

## Identify the Pitches

What is the first pitch of "All Around the Buttercup"? What pitch ends the first phrase? What pitch ends the second phrase?

# A GAME to PLAY

## Playing the Buttercup Game

- Form a circle and hold hands.
- Raise your arms to make "windows."
- The leader moves around the circle, weaving in and out of the windows.

# Pentatonic Calypso

"Cookie" is a pentatonic song in the calypso style. **Listen** to the song. **Sing** the responses. Then **sing** the calls.

6–5

## Cookie

*Calypso Song from the West Indies*

Cook-ie, you sure no-bod-y passed here?    No, my friend.

Cook-ie, you sure no-bod-y passed here?    No, my friend.    Well!

One of me dump-lin's gone! Don't tell ___ me so!

One of me dump-lin's gone! Don't tell ___ me so!

One of me dump-lin's gone!    Aw!

## Meet *do* Pentatonic

"Cookie" is a *do*-pentatonic song because it has five different pitches and it ends on *do*. What are the other pitches?

## Sing *do* Pentatonic

**Sing** the calls with pitch syllables as your partner sings the responses with pitch syllables. **Play** this rhythm during the responses on the first and second lines.

Calypso music originally came from Trinidad. Some instruments used in calypso music are steel drums, guitar, and maracas.

# Playing a Button Game

Have you ever lost something? Where did you find it? **Sing** this "lost and found" song and play the game.

6–7

## Button, You Must Wander

*Traditional Game Song from the United States*

But - ton, you must wan - der, wan - der, wan - der,

But - ton, you must wan - der ev - 'ry - where;

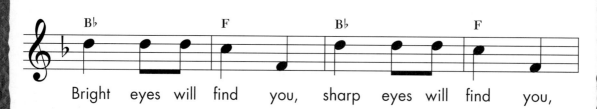

Bright eyes will find you, sharp eyes will find you,

But - ton, you must wan - der ev - 'ry - where.

## Add Instruments

Choose a melody instrument. **Play** this accompaniment as the class sings the song. Which instrument will you choose?

*(Play only on phrases 1, 2, and 4)*

# Show What You Know!

These are phrases from familiar songs.
**Sing** the phrases with pitch syllables.
Name each song.

1.

2.

3.

4.

# Sounds of Dixieland

New Orleans was one of the early homes of Dixieland jazz. Woodwind and brass instruments are an important part of this style of music. **Listen** to the song. What instruments do you hear?

6–8 *When the Saints Go Marching In*

*African American Spiritual*

1. Oh, when the saints _____ go march-ing in, _____

Oh, when the saints go march - ing in, _____

Oh, Lord I want to be in that num - ber _____

When the saints go march - ing in.

2. Oh, when the stars
   refuse to shine, . . .

3. Oh, when I hear
   that trumpet sound, . . .

# A Jazz Great

**Listen** to Louis Armstrong's performance of *When the Saints Go Marching In.* What instruments do you hear?

6–9

## When the Saints Go Marching In

**Traditional Dixieland Tune**

Louis Armstrong's audiences loved this song. They often asked him to perform it.

## M·U·S·I·C  M·A·K·E·R·S

*Louis Armstrong*

**Louis Armstrong** (1900–1971) was born in New Orleans. His nickname was "Satchmo." He was a trumpet player, singer, and band leader. Louis Armstrong is one of the most important people in the history of jazz.

# Hear a Little Salsa!

"*Cheki, morena*" is a singing game from Puerto Rico. **Listen** to the song. Which instruments can you **identify**? Now **sing** the song and play the game.

6–10

## Cheki, morena
### (Shake It!)

*English Words by Alice D. Firgau*  *Singing Game from Puerto Rico*

Che - ki mo - re - na, che - ki,
Shake it, come on now, shake it!

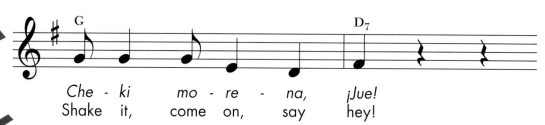

Che - ki mo - re - na, ¡Jue!
Shake it, come on, say hey!

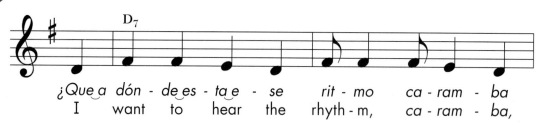

¿Que a dón - de es - ta e - se rit - mo ca - ram - ba
I want to hear the rhyth - m, ca - ram - ba,

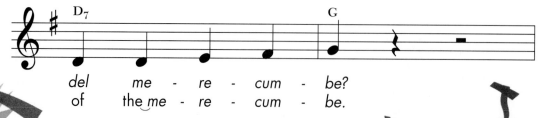

del me - re - cum - be?
of the me - re - cum - be.

176

# Salsa!

**Listen** to *Vaya Puente*. What instruments do you hear? This style of music is called *salsa*.

6–14
## Vaya Puente

**by Tito Puente**

The solo on this recording is played on a trombone.

Un pa - si - to a - lan - te
Take a little step for - ward,

Yo - tro pa - ra tras
Take a little step back,

Y dan - do la vuel - ta dan - do la vuel - ta
and turn - ing a - round and turn - ing a - round you

¿Quién se que - da - ra? ¡Jue!
know you've got the knack. Hey!

# A New Kind of Ostinato

**Sing** this folk song and learn to play the game. To begin, form a circle with one person in the middle.

6–15

## The Farmer's Dairy Key

*Folk Song from the United States*

1. I lost the far - mer's dai - ry key,

I'm in this la - dy's gar - den.

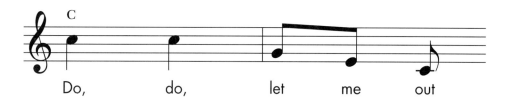

Do, do, let me out

I'm in this la - dy's gar - den.

2. A brass key and a silver lock, . . .

3. A corn stalk fiddle and shoe string bow, . . .

**Video Library** Watch *One Voice, Many Voices*. Listen to another song with melodic ostinatos.

## Ostinato with a Melody

When an ostinato has a melody, it is called a melodic ostinato. **Sing** this melodic ostinato as the rest of the class sings the song. **Describe** the texture. How many layers are there?

# Putting It

## What Do You Know?

Read the pitches in the song "Cookie" on page 170.

**a.** Find all the pitches called *so*.

**b.** Find all the pitches called *la*.

**c.** Find all the pitches called *mi*.

**d.** Find all the pitches called *re*.

**e.** Find all the notes called *do*.

6–17

## What Do You Hear? 5

You will hear four musical examples. Decide which instrument is playing in each example.

**1.**

**2.**

**3.**

**4.**

# All Together

## Perform Rhythms

Say these rhythm patterns, using rhythm syllables.

a.

b.

c.

## Create an Accompaniment

Choose one of the rhythms above. Play it with "The Farmer's Dairy Key" on page 178.

- What instrument will you use to play your accompaniment?

- How many times will you need to play the pattern to accompany the song?

## Create a Dance

Create a new way to do the "Dinosaur Dance" on page 166. Move one way for the **A** section and a different way for the **B** section.

## Stampin' to the Beat

Jazz is a style of music. Jazz invites musicians to make each song they perform their own.

**Listen** to the *The Flat Foot Floogee*. Feel the beat and stamp your right foot on the first beat of each measure.

**6–21**
**The Flat Foot Floogee**

**by Slim Gaillard, Slam Stewart, and Bud Green**

A recording of this song was placed in a time capsule at the 1939 World's Fair. It will be opened in the year 5000.

# Making Music Our Own

## Singing with Style

Now **sing** the song in your own way.
You can change the dynamics, use accents,
or sing *staccato* or *legato*. What other
ways can you make this song your own?

 **6–22** The Flat Foot Floogee

*Words and Music by Slim Gaillard,
Slam Stewart, and Bud Green*

The flat foot floo-gee with the floy floy, —
The flat foot floo-gee with the flou* flou, —

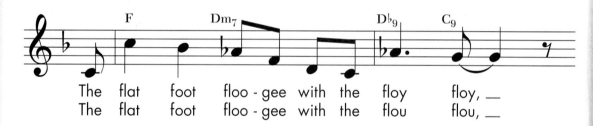

The flat foot floo-gee with the floy floy, —
The flat foot floo-gee with the flou flou, —

The flat foot floo-gee with the floy floy, —
The flat foot floo-gee with the flou flou, —

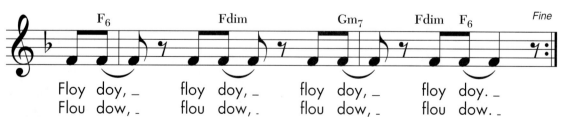

Floy doy, _ floy doy, _ floy doy, _ floy doy. _
Flou dow, _ flou dow, _ flou dow, _ flou dow. _

*Rhymes with "how"

184

If you're feel-in' low-down,    Don't know what to do, ___

*D.C. al Fine*

And you want a    show-down,    Here's the on-ly    dance for you. ___

# M·U·S·I·C   M·A·K·E·R·S

## "Slim" Gaillard and "Slam" Stewart

**Bulee "Slim" Gaillard** (1916–1991) and **Leroy "Slam" Stewart** (1914–1987) were known for their own style of high-energy jazz. They first met in New York City in 1936. "Slam" had already developed his own fun jazz style. The team was known as "Slim and Slam." They were popular on the top radio shows of the day.

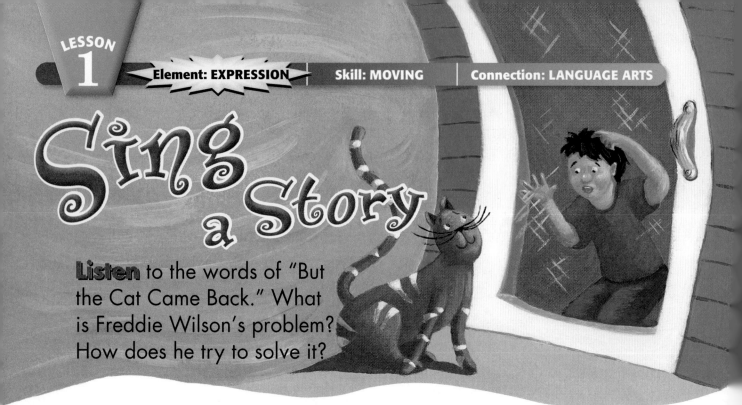

# Sing a Story

**Listen** to the words of "But the Cat Came Back." What is Freddie Wilson's problem? How does he try to solve it?

6–24

## But the Cat Came Back
*Words and Music by Josef Marais*

VERSE

*p* 1. Fred-die Wil-son had a cat that he did-n't want to keep.

He of-fered him for free and he tried to sell him cheap.

He called up-on the preach-er one Sun-day for ad-vice;

The preach-er said, "Yes, leave him here, it would be so nice!"

# Soft, Loud, . . . Hold!

Now **sing** the verses softly and the refrain loudly.

Find the note with the **fermata** and hold it for a long time with your whole body. Then decide how to **move** to the refrain.

A **fermata** ⌢ tells a performer to hold a note for an extra long time.

*f* But the cat came back, he would-n't stay a - way,

He was sit - tin' on the porch on the ver - y next day.

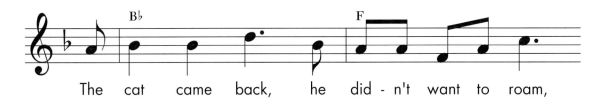

The cat came back, he did - n't want to roam,

The ver - y next day it was "Home, Sweet Home."

2. Freddie put him on a ship and they headed for Ceylon.
The ship was overloaded more than twenty thousand ton.
Not far away from shore the cargo ship went down,
There wasn't any doubt about it, everybody drowned.  *Refrain*

3. Then he put the cat aboard with a man in a balloon,
Who would give the cat away to the man in the moon.
The balloon it didn't rise, it burst in bits instead,
And ten miles from the spot, they found the man stone dead.  *Refrain*

# Rhythms in Three

**Listen** to *"Caballito blanco."* How many beats are in each measure? Which is the strongest beat?

**Listen** to *"Caballito blanco"* again. Use this pattern to keep the steady beat.

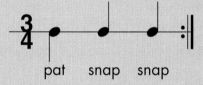

$\frac{3}{4}$

pat   snap   snap

## Your Own Three-Beat Pattern

**Create** other ways to play the three-beat pattern. **Play** your pattern as you sing the song.

# Caballito blanco
## (Little White Pony)

English Words by Bryan Louiselle

Folk Song from Mexico

1. Ca - ba - lli - to     blan - co,
1. Take  me,  dear   white    po - ny,

sá - ca - me     de a    quí. _____
Take   me   far    a - way, _____

Llé - va - me a    mi     pueb - lo
Back   to    my   own    vil - lage

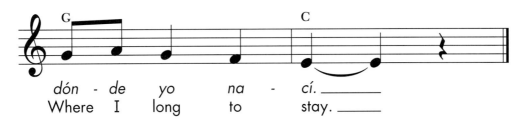

dón - de    yo    na - cí. _____
Where  I   long    to    stay. _____

2. Tengo, tengo, tengo,
   tu no tienes nada.
   Tengo tres borregas
   en una manada.

2. I have quite a fortune,
   You don't have a penny.
   I've three lambs to care for;
   You do not have any.

3. Una me da leche,
   otra me da lana,
   Y otra mantequilla,
   para la semana.

   Repeat verse 1

3. One gives milk each morning,
   One provides her wool,
   One whose gift of butter
   Keeps the larder full.

   Repeat verse 1

**Element: RHYTHM** | **Skill: MOVING** | **Connection: CULTURE**

# Moving in Twos and Threes

Lullabies are soft, gentle songs that people sing to help babies sleep. "Boysie" is a lullaby from Trinidad, an island in the Caribbean Sea.

Pretend you are rocking a baby to sleep. As you **listen** to the song, sway left and right on the strong beats. How many beats do you feel before you sway again?

**Left**

1  2  3

**Right**

1  2  3

# Lullaby in Three

As you **sing** "Boysie," **tap** your feet lightly.
Feel the pattern of three beats in each measure.

6–29

## Boysie

*Lullaby from Trinidad*

Rock,    a rock, a rock, Boy - sie,    Boy - sie  can't sleep;

Rock,    a rock, a rock, Boy - sie,    Boy - sie  can't sleep.

*Fine*

Look    up - town, look    down - town,  find  Boy - sie    there;

Look    up - hill, look    down - hill,  find  Boy - sie    there.

*D.C. al Fine*

# Lullaby in Two

"Sleep, Baby, Sleep" is another lullaby. It is in **meter** in two. What is the meter of "Boysie?"

**Move** with streamers to show the meter of "Sleep, Baby, Sleep."

**Meter** is the way the beats of music are grouped together. They are often in sets of two or sets of three.

## Time to Sleep

As you **sing** "Sleep, Baby, Sleep," pretend to rock a baby.

**6–31**

### Sleep, Baby, Sleep

*Lullaby*
*Adapted by Cheryl Warren-Mattox*

*do*

1. Sleep,     sleep,     ba - by     sleep, _____
2. Sleep,     sleep,     ba - by     sleep, _____

Go     through     dream - land's     path.
Do     just     as     I     say.

But     I     warn     you,     yes ___ I     do,
Go     to     sleep,     sleep,     ba - by     sleep,

That     the     tor - toise     is     ver - y     near.
And     the     tor - toise     will     go     a - way.

Yes     the     tor - toise     is     ver - y     near. _____
Yes     the     tor - toise     will     go     a - way. _____

3. Sleep, sleep, baby sleep,
Dream sweet dreams.
You are safe, Mommy is here,
I will always be very near.
Yes I'll always be very near.

# One, Two, Three, Read!

"*Un, deux, trois*" is a traditional clapping game from France. **Sing** the song and play the game that goes with it!

**6-35**

## Un, deux, trois

**(One, Two, Three)**     *Singing Game from France*

Un,   deux,   trois   main   droite.
One,   two,   three   right   hand.

Un,   deux,   trois   main   gauche.
One,   two,   three   left   hand.

Un,   deux,   trois   main   droite,   main   gauche   et
One,   two,   three   right   hand,   left   hand   and

1.
un,   deux,   trois   les   deux.
one,   two,   three   both   hands.

2.
un,   deux,   trois   les   deux.
one,   two,   three   both   hands.

## Read the Song

*"Un, deux, trois"* has three rhythms that you know: ♩, ♫, and 𝄽.

**Read** the song with rhythm syllables.

Here are two rhythm patterns to accompany *"Un, deux, trois."* **Play** one of the patterns as the class sings the song.

# Sing It Again

When you **sing** "Shoo, Fly," there is a special thing you need to do. When you get to the end of the song, you will see the words **D.C. al Fine.** What do you do?

**D.C. al Fine** is an Italian phrase that tells you to go back to the beginning of the song and sing until the word *Fine* [FEE-neh].

6–39

## Shoo, Fly

*Folk Song from the United States*

Shoo, fly, don't both - er me, Shoo, fly, don't both - er me,

Shoo, fly, don't both - er me, For I be - long to some-bod - y.

I feel, I feel, I feel, I feel like a morn-ing star,

I feel, I feel, I feel, I feel, I feel like a morn-ing star. So,

196

# A New Form

After you **sing** "Shoo, Fly," decide which picture shows the form of the song.

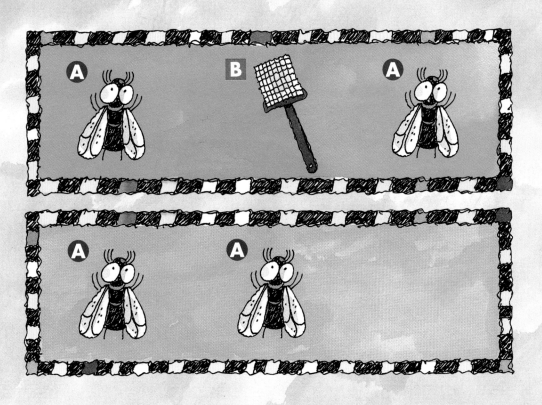

# Flies

*by Dorothy Aldis*

Flies walk on ceilings
And straight up the walls
Not even the littlest
Fly ever falls.

And I am quite certain
If *I* were a fly
I'd leave my home to go
Walk on the sky.

Have you ever had shoo fly pie? Traditionally, Amish children are assigned "guard duty" to shoo away flies as the pie cools on the window sill.

# A Mountain of a FORM

This song has one section, **A**. Sing the song to discover its message.

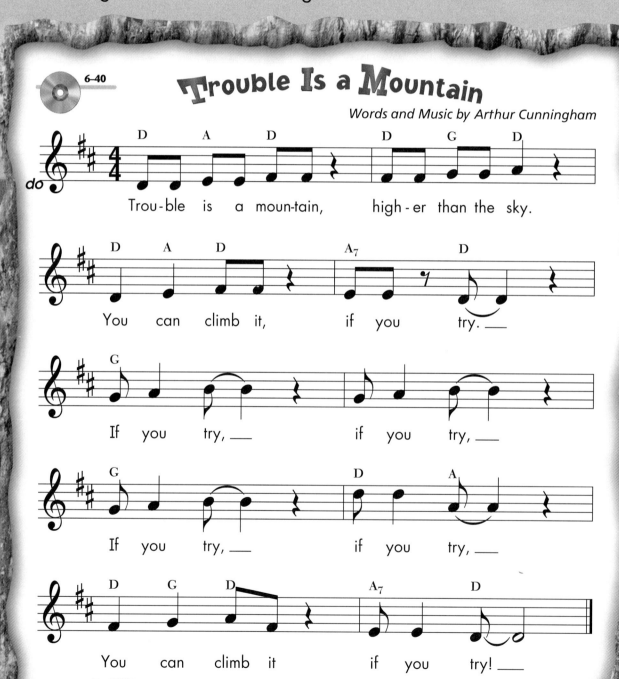

6–40

## Trouble Is a Mountain

*Words and Music by Arthur Cunningham*

Trou-ble is a moun-tain, high-er than the sky.

You can climb it, if you try. ___

If you try, ___ if you try, ___

If you try, ___ if you try, ___

You can climb it if you try! ___

## Beyond ABA Form

**Create** new music to play after singing the song and call it **B**. What would you call the form of the music now?

Create more new music and call it **C**. Then **perform** the music in this order.

- Sing the song.
- Play the **B** music.
- Sing the song again.
- Play the **C** music.
- Sing the song.

How would you **describe** the new form?

## M·U·S·I·C  M·A·K·E·R·S

### Arthur Cunningham

**Arthur Cunningham** (1928–1997) was a composer and teacher. His students loved him very much. He believed you can do anything if you try hard enough. Cunningham wrote the song "Trouble Is a Mountain" for the students at Upper Nyack Elementary School in New York.

# Pitches in the House

**Sing** "Great Big House." How many different pitches are in the song?

7–1

## Great Big House

*Play-Party Song from Louisiana*

do

Great big house in New Or-leans, For-ty sto-ries high, ___

Eve-ry room that I've been in, Filled with pump-kin pie.

2. Went down to the old mill stream
   To fetch a pail of water;
   Put one arm around my wife,
   The other 'round my daughter.

3. Fare thee well, my darling girl,
   Fare thee well, my daughter;
   Fare thee well, my darling girl,
   With golden slippers on her.

re

do

# Pentatonic House

The five different pitches in "Great Big House" are shown on the staff below. On what pitch does the song end? This pitch is called the home tone.

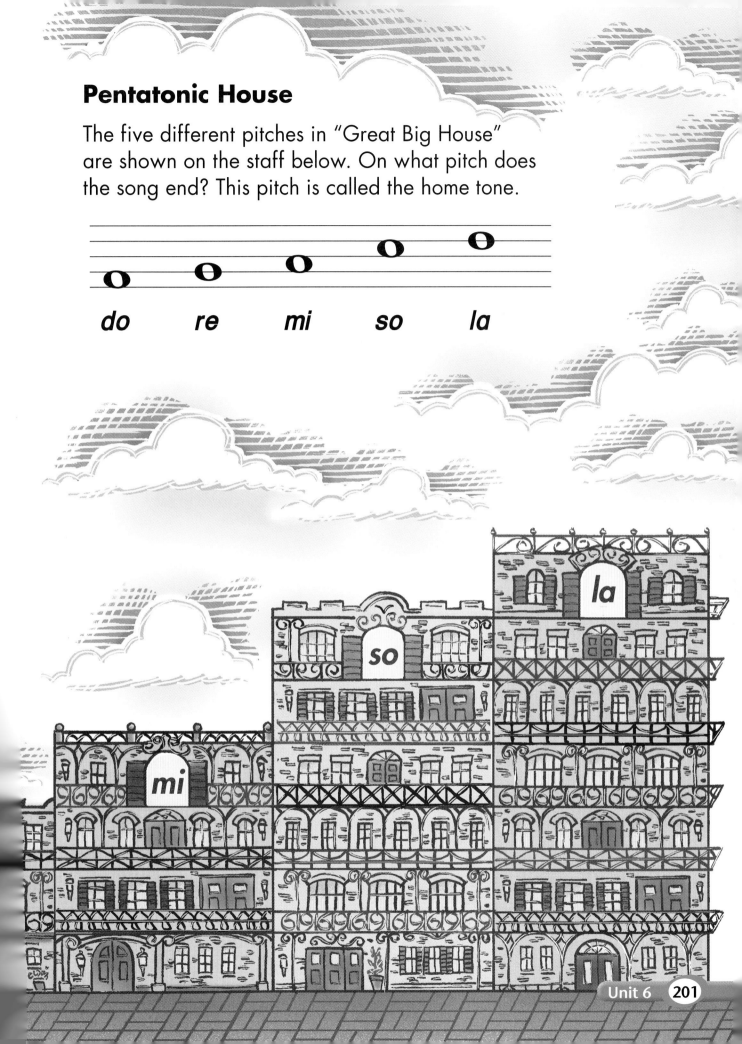

do    re    mi    so    la

# Sing It Again!

Now **sing** "Great Big House" with pitch syllables and hand signs.

# Mystery Melodies

Solve this mystery. **Sing** these melodies with pitch syllables. Then see if you can name each song.

1. do do do  mi mi mi mi  so so so la so mi do  mi  re  do

2. mi re do re  mi so re  do  re  mi  mi re do re  mi so re  mi  re  do

# Show What You Know!

**Create** your own *do*-pentatonic melody. Choose one of the rhythms below. Make sure your melody ends on *do*, the home tone.

Write your melody on a staff and teach it to a partner.

**Sing** "See-Saw Sacradown." What happens to the melody on the words *up* and *down*?

*7–5*

## See-Saw Sacradown

*Traditional Rhyme*

*Music by Paul Kapp*

See - Saw    Sac - ra - down,

Which is the way to Lon - don town?

One foot up, the oth - er foot down,

That is the way to Lon - don town.

# Add an Ostinato

**Play** this melodic ostinato with "See-Saw Sacradown."

Xylophone

# Play a Pentatonic Melody

**Play** "See-Saw Sacradown." Here are the pitches you need.

D E G A B D E G A

## Tune In

"See-Saw Sacradown" is a Mother Goose rhyme. Children have used this rhyme to keep time on a see-saw.

# Melody Train

**Listen** to "Chicka Hanka," an African American work song. Then **sing** the song.

## Play an Ostinato

**Play** this melodic ostinato as the class sings the song.

Xylophone

When two trains use the same track, sometimes one has to take the "side track" and wait for the other to pass.

# Chicka Hanka

African American Work Song

*Call*

Cap - tain, go side - track your train! _

*Response*        *Fine*

Chick - a hank - a, chick - a hank - a, chick - a hank - a, chick - a

*Call*

Cap - tain, go side - track your train! _

hank - a.

*Response*

Chick - a hank - a, chick - a hank - a, chick - a hank - a, chick - a

*Call*        *D.C. al Fine*

Num - ber three in line a - com - in' in on time.

hank - a.

# Plugged-in Sound

Some instruments depend on electricity for sound. Can you name any?

The theremin was one of the first electronic instruments. It was created about 1919 by a Russian inventor, Leon Theremin. It can make spooky music, like the kind you hear in scary movies.

Listen to Lydia Kavina playing *Free Music #1*.

**7-9**

## Free Music #1

**by Percy Grainger**

Kavina controls the sound of the theremin by moving her hands over two antennae.

## M·U·S·I·C  M·A·K·E·R·S

### Lydia Kavina

**Lydia Kavina** (born 1967) came from Russia. She began studying with Leon Theremin when she was nine years old and started giving concerts when she was 14. Now she is one of the leading theremin players in the world.

▲ Lydia Kavina, age 9, with Leon Theremin.

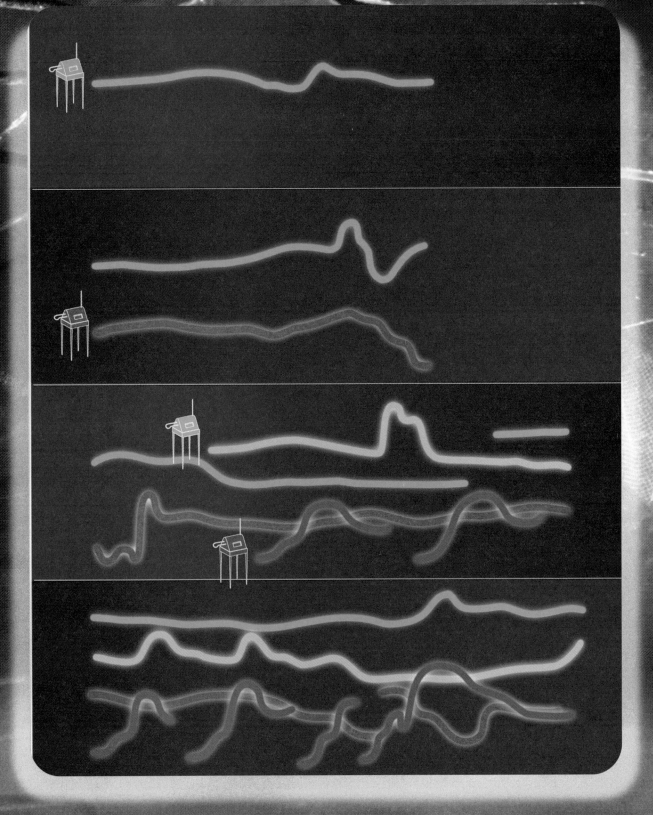

**Electronic Keyboard** Experiment with different sounds on a synthesizer. Invent interesting ways to combine sounds.

# LOTS AND LOTS

**Play** this accompaniment as the class sings "Rosie, Darling Rosie." Notice how your hands move together to play this ostinato.

Bass Xylophone

## Rhythm Texture

**Play** the rhythm of the words on these instruments to make a thicker texture.

Ro - sie, dar-ling Ro - sie

Ha - ha, Ro - sie

Can I play the conga?

# OF LAYERS

## Rosie, Darling Rosie

*African American Game Song*

*Solo*

1. Ro - sie, dar - ling Ro - sie, Ha - ha, Ro - sie;
2. Ro - sie, dar - ling Ro - sie, Ha - ha, Ro - sie;

*Solo*

Ro - sie, dar - ling Ro - sie, Ha - ha, Ro - sie;
Ro - sie, dar - ling Ro - sie, Ha - ha, Ro - sie;

*Solo*

Way down yon - der in Bal - ti - more, — Ha - ha, Ro - sie;
Come a - long — and fol-low me, — Ha - ha, Ro - sie;

*Solo*

Need no car - pet on my floor, — Ha - ha, Ro - sie.
Let's go down to Gal - i - lee, — Ha - ha, Ro - sie.

# Create a

There is an African story called *The Animals Find Water*. In it, a lion helps the jungle animals dig a well. First he dances while the drummer plays. When he gets tired, he encourages the other animals to take his place. As the animals take turns dancing, the hole gets deeper and deeper until finally, water comes gushing forth!

**Create** a play of the story with your class.

# Lion's Tale

## Sing the Lion's Song

Here is a song you can **sing** as part of the play.

**7–12**

# Kou ri lengay
### (The Strength of the Lion)

Words by Ague Commari

Game Song from Tanzania

Kou ri len - gay! Ka - len - gan - a chum, chum, pah!

Kou ri len - gay! Ka - len - gan - a chum, chum, pah!

Kou ri len - gay! Ka - len - gan - a chum, chum, pah!

Kou ri len - gay! Ka - len - gan - a chum, chum, pah!

*Four times*

O the strength of the li - on is in his tail.

# Jungle Rhythms

Here are two ostinatos you can **play** to accompany *"Kou ri lengay."*

Mon-key, mon-key, danc - ing.

Great     gray     el - e - phant.

Now **create** an ostinato of your own to accompany the song.

## Jungle Textures

To add another layer to the accompaniment, **play** this ostinato on a xylophone.

Now **improvise** another layer, using only the pitches shown below.

To **improvise** means to make up music as it is being performed.

# Putting It

## What Do You Know?

**1.** Match the following words with the correct definitions.

**a.** *fermata*

**b.** *do* pentatonic

**c.** *D.C. al Fine*

• Go back to the beginning of the song and sing until the word *Fine*.

• Hold a note for an extra long time.

• A song that ends on *do* and has five different pitches

**2.** Read each rhythm pattern below. Find the number of beats in each pattern.

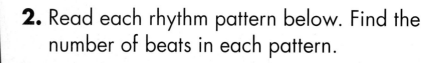

## What Do You Hear? 6

7–15

Listen to the three musical examples. Which set of symbols shows the form of the music?

**1.** Ⓐ Ⓑ Ⓐ    Ⓐ Ⓑ

**2.** Ⓐ Ⓑ Ⓐ    Ⓐ Ⓑ

**3.** Ⓐ Ⓑ Ⓐ    Ⓐ Ⓑ

# All Together

## What You Can Do

### Sing a Melody

Find the song "Great Big House" on page 200. Sing one verse of the song, using pitch syllables and hand signs.

### Play an Ostinato

Now play the following ostinato as an accompaniment for "Great Big House."

### Create a New Section

Improvise a four-measure **B** section for "Great Big House." Use the pitches shown below. What rhythms will you use?

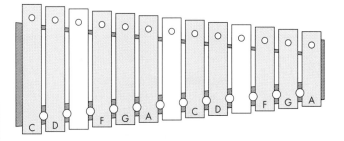

# PATHS TO MAKING MUSIC

# Sights and Sounds of American Music

In these pictures, musicians are playing many different kinds of music. Talk about what you see. As you **listen**, match the music you hear with the pictures.

7–20

**American Music Styles Sound Montage**

Bluegrass

# Music USA

In the United States, people enjoy music from all over the world. What kinds of music do you like?

# Many Kinds of Music

**Sing** this song. Listen for musical sounds from around the world.

 7–18

## Ev'ry Kind of Music

*Words and Music by David Eddleman*

Ev'-'ry kind of mu - sic,     Got-ta have mu - sic,

Give me lots of mu - sic     to sing and dance and play. ____

Feel the beat a-mov - in',     Sing-in' a song to make my day,

Makes me swing and sway sing-in' on the way. ____

## America Loves Music

People show how they like music in different ways. How does the person in this poem express her feelings about music?

### Way Down in the Music

*by Eloise Greenfield*

I get way down in the music
Down inside the music
I let it wake me
      Take me
Spin me around and make me
Uh—get down

I get way down in the music
Down inside the music
I let it wake me
      Take me
Spin me around and shake me
I get down, down
I get down

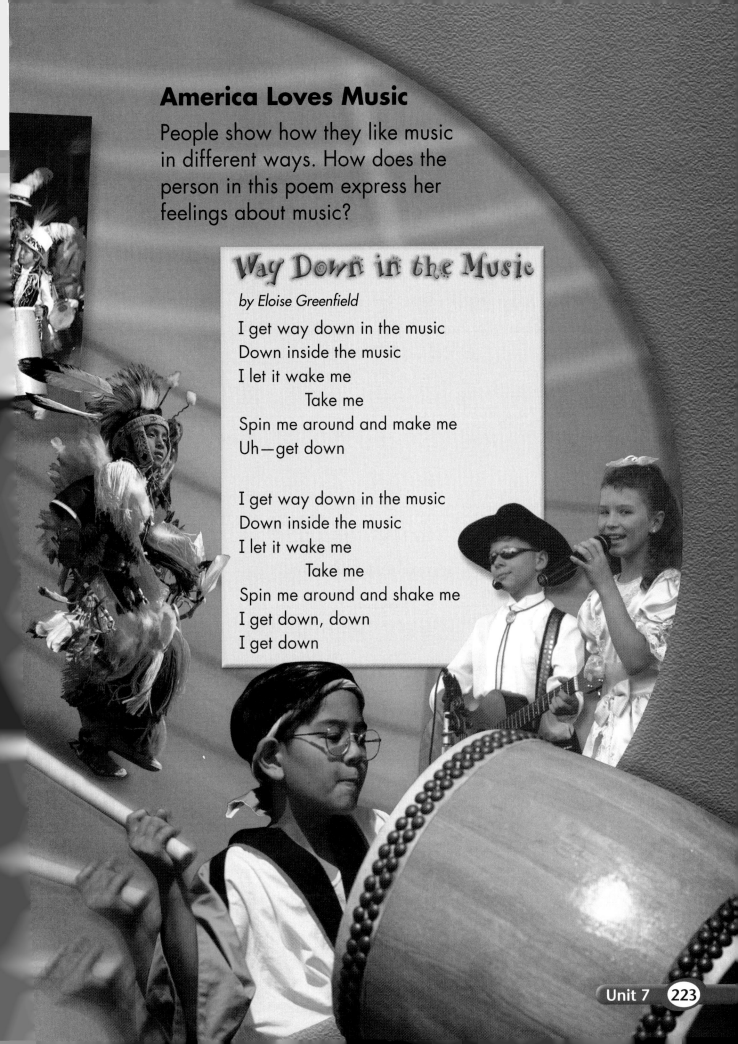

# FRIENDS Around the Country

Friends share their ideas and feelings.
**Sing** this song about friends cooperating to try new things.

7-21

## Glad to Have a Friend Like You

*Words and Music by Carol Hall*

VERSE

1. Jill told Bill that it was lots of fun to cook.

Bill told Jill that she could bait a real fish-hook.

So they made oo - ey goo - ey choc - olate
And they sat by the riv - er and they

cake stick - y lick - y sug - ar
fished in the wa - ter and they

top and they gob - bled it and gig - gled.
talked as the squirm - y worm - ies wig - gled.

**REFRAIN**

Sing - in', Glad to have a friend like you,

fair, and fun, and skip - pin' free.

Glad to have a friend like you, and

glad to just be me.

2. Peg told Greg she liked to make things out of chairs.
   Greg told Peg sometimes he still hugged teddy bears.
   So they sneaked in the living room and piled all the pillows up and
   Made it a rocket ship to fly in.
   And the bears were their girls and boys and they were the astronauts
   Who lived on the moon with one pet lion.
   *Refrain*

## Free to Be . . .

Talk about the kinds of things you like to do with your friends. What makes your friends special to you?

## Create a Verse

Think of two names that rhyme. Use them to **create** a new verse that fits the rhythm of "Glad to Have a Friend Like You."

Tune In

Free to Be . . . You and Me is an Emmy Award-winning television show. "Glad to Have a Friend Like You" is a song from this show.

# Together and Strong

There are many songs about friendship. **Listen** to *Stick Together*. How does this song express the ways friends can help one another?

7–23

## Stick Together

**by John McCutcheon and Si Kahn**

When John McCutcheon was a young boy he loved music and baseball. As an adult he has been successful in both music and baseball.

**CD-ROM** Use music notation software to create a rhythm accompaniment for "Glad to Have a Friend Like You."

# Games Americans Play

Folk songs and games are passed down by families and friends. One person teaches another how to sing the song or play the game. Then that person teaches someone else. "Bob-a-Needle" is an African American singing game played in a circle.

7–24

## Bob-a-Needle

*African American Ring Game*

Bob - a - need - le, bob - a - need - le is a - run - ning.

Bob - a - need - le, bob - a - need - le is a run - ning,

Bet - ter hide, bob - a - need - le, bob - a - need - le is a run - ning,

Bet - ter hus - tle, bob - a - need - le, bob - a - need - le is a run - ning,

I'll catch bob - a - need - le, bob - a - need - le's not a run - ning.

# Play the Bob-a-Needle Game

Play the game as you **sing** the song. Each time you repeat the game, sing and **move** at a faster tempo.

# Singing on the Texas Trail

Years ago, it took a very long time for cowhands to drive cattle along a trail from Texas to Kansas. They sang songs like this one to pass the time.

7–26

## The Big Corral

*Cowboy Song from the United States*

The hus - ky brute from the cat - tle chute,

Press a-long to the big cor - ral!

He should be brand - ed on the snoot,

Press a-long to the big cor - ral!

## Arts Connection

◄ *Untitled* by N.C. Wyeth

Here is a scene from a day in the life of a cowboy.

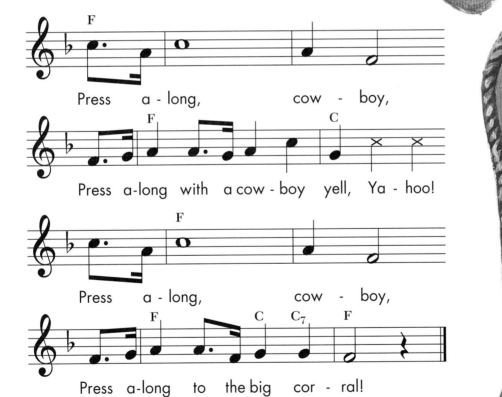

Press a - long, cow - boy,

Press a-long with a cow - boy yell, Ya - hoo!

Press a - long, cow - boy,

Press a-long to the big cor - ral!

# Play Along the Trail

**Play** these patterns as the class sings.
Be sure to keep a steady beat.

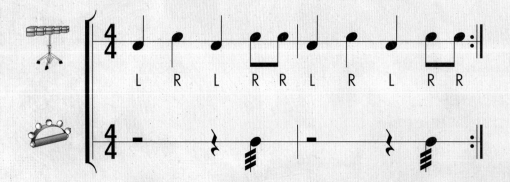

L  L  R  L  R  R  L  R  L  R  R

What kinds of sounds would cowboys hear on
the trail? Now **create** your own trail sounds.

## More Cowboy Music

**Listen** to *The Big Country*. Find the parts
in the listening map where the cowboys
are moving the cattle as fast as they can.
Then find the parts where they are resting.

**7–27**
**The Big Country**

**by Jerome Moross**
*The Big Country* was the theme music for
a cowboy movie made in 1958.

# The Big Country
## Listening Map

**Scene 1**

**Scene 2**

**Scene 3**

**Scene 4**

# TWO American Styles

This singing game dates back to the late 1800s. **Sing** the song, then learn the game.

 7–28

## A-Tisket, A-Tasket

*Folk Song from the United States*

A - tis - ket, a - tas - ket, a green and yel - low bas - ket,

I wrote a let - ter to my love and on the way I lost it,

I lost it, I lost it, and on the way I lost it,

a lit - tle dog - gie picked it up and put it in his pock - et.

# Jazzin' Up a Song

**Listen** to this version of "A-Tisket, A-Tasket."

**Compare** the singing styles in both recordings.

7–30
## A-Tisket, A-Tasket

**Folk Song from the United States as adapted and sung by Ella Fitzgerald**

Fitzgerald first sang her jazz version of "A-Tisket, A-Tasket" when she was only 18 years old.

### M·U·S·I·C  M·A·K·E·R·S
## Ella Fitzgerald

**Ella Fitzgerald** (1918–1996) started making music when she was a child. People loved hearing her sing. She became very famous and sang jazz all over the world. She once starred in a television commercial where she sang a note that broke a crystal glass.

# shining from the Inside

When something makes you very happy, you "shine"! Why are the people in these photos "shining"? As you **sing** this song, think about something that makes you "shine."

7–31

## We're All Gonna Shine Tonight

*Camp Song from the United States*

We're all gon-na shine to-night, we're all gon-na shine.

We're all gon-na shine to-night, all down the line.

We're all dressed up to-night; we're feel - ing fine. When the

sun goes down and the moon comes up, We're all gon-na shine.

## Shining Sounds

Choose instruments that have a "shining" sound.
Here are some rhythm patterns to **play**.

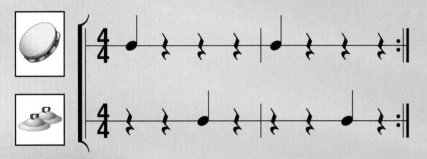

## Let Your Light Shine

**Listen** to this African American spiritual.
How do you let your light shine?

7-33
**This Little Light of Mine**

**Traditional African American**

This song celebrates everyone's special qualities.

# Express Yourself

What feelings are expressed in this spiritual? **Sing** "I Got Shoes." Use dynamics, such as *crescendos*, to express the feelings of the song.

7–34

## I Got Shoes

African American Spiritual

*Swing Style*
*Solo*

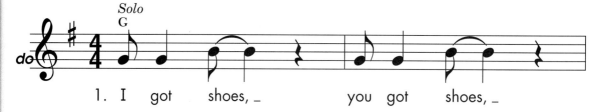

1. I got shoes, _ you got shoes, _

All God's chil - dren got shoes;

*Chorus*

When I get to heav-en, gon-na put on my shoes; _ I'm gon-na

walk all o - ver God's heav - en, _____

Heav - en, _____  Heav - en; _____

Ev - 'ry - bod - y  talk - in' 'bout  heav - en ain't  go - in' there,

Heav - en, _____  Heav - en, _____  Gon - na

walk  all  o - ver God's  heav - en. _____

2.  I got a song, you got a song,
    All God's children got a song;
    When I get to heaven,
       gonna sing my song;
    I'm gonna sing
       all over God's heaven, . . .
    Gonna sing all over God's heaven.

3.  I got wings, you got wings,
    All God's children got wings;
    When I get to heaven,
       gonna put on my wings;
    I'm gonna fly
       all over God's heaven, . . .
    Gonna fly all over God's heaven.

# TEXAS Play-Party

Long before radio, television, and movies, people got together and danced for entertainment. These dances were called play-parties.

**Sing** this play-party from Texas.

8–1

## Shake Them 'Simmons Down

*Play-Party Song from Texas*

1. Cir - cle right, do - oh, do - oh,
2. Cir - cle left, do - oh, do - oh,

Cir - cle right, do - oh, do - oh,
Cir - cle left, do - oh, do - oh,

Cir - cle right, do - oh, do - oh,
Cir - cle left, do - oh, do - oh,

Shake them 'sim - mons down.

3. Boys to the center, do-oh, do-oh, . . .  5. Promenade all, do-oh, do-oh, . . .

4. Girls to the center, do-oh, do-oh, . . .  6. Swing your corner, do-oh, do-oh, . . .

## Shake and Sing

The percussion instruments below are played by shaking them. Choose an instrument. Take turns playing it while the class sings the song. You can **play** a steady beat or the rhythm of words.

**Fruit Shakers**          **Maracas**

## You Can Dance

"Shake Them 'Simmons Down" is a play-party dance you can learn.

# Music from Puerto Rico

Flowers love to grow in the warm and sunny climate of Puerto Rico. Spanish is the main language spoken in Puerto Rico, an island in the Caribbean Sea. Did you know that it is part of the United States?

**Sing** "El florón," a game from Puerto Rico.

8–4

## El florón (The Flower)

*English Words by Verne Muñoz*          *Singing Game from Puerto Rico*

**A**

do

El flo - rón    pas - ó    por    a - quí,
Pass   the   flow - er   round and   a - round.

Yo   no   lo   vi,    Yo   no   lo   vi.
Will   it   be   found?   Will   it   be   found?

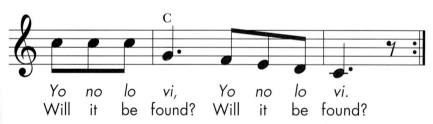

**B**

Que   pa - se,    que   pa - se,
Where  is        it?   Where  is        it?

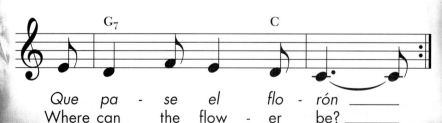

Que   pa - se   el    flo - rón _____
Where can    the   flow - er   be? _____

## The Flower Game

Play this circle game with a flower.
**Move** one way for the **A** section.
Move a different way for the **B** section.

## Puerto Rico—*Salsa!*

*Salsa* is a combination of American jazz and Cuban and Puerto Rican dance music. **Listen** to *Loco bossa nova*. How would you **move** to this music?

**8–8**

### Loco bossa nova

**by Tito Puente**
The drums featured on this recording are called *timbales* [tihm-BAH-lehs].

# Music of the First Americans

Each Native American tribe in the United States has its own music.

**Sing** this song of the Wechihit-Yokuts of California. They believe that the eagle is the most powerful of all birds.

8–9

## Song of the Eagle

*Native American Song of the Wechihit*

Heh - weh - yeh kah - ah - wah

Heh - weh - yeh kah - wah

ah wah - kah - ah chah_ choh - cheh leh mah nohn.

# Powwow Dance

**Move** to the steady beat as you sing "Duck Dance." This Choctaw and Seminole song is performed at powwows.

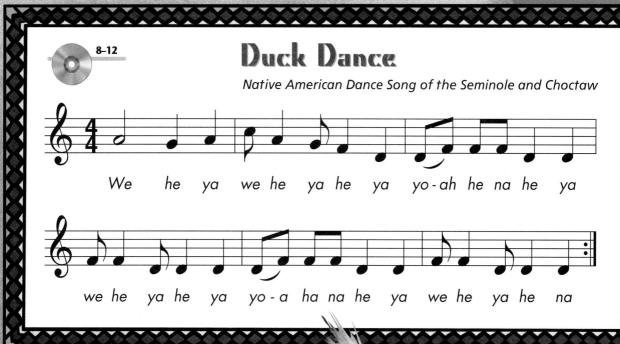

**8–12**

## Duck Dance

*Native American Dance Song of the Seminole and Choctaw*

We    he    ya    we he    ya he    ya    yo-ah he na he    ya

we he    ya he    ya    yo-a    ha na he    ya    we he    ya he    na

The Snake Dance is a Florida Seminole stomp dance. ▶

# Rock 'n' Roll USA

In the 1960s, rock and roll music was at the top of the pop charts. It had a new and fresh sound. **Listen** to the song "Peppermint Twist." **Describe** what you hear.

## Peppermint Twist

8–15

*Words and Music by Henry Glover and Joey Dee*

They  got  a new dance and  it  goes like  this. _
Meet _ me,  pal, down on  forty - fifth  street _

The  name  of the dance _  is  the Pep - per-mint Twist. _
Where the _ Pep - per-mint _  Twist - ers meet, _

Well, you'll like _____ it  like  this, _ the Pep-per-mint Twist.
And  you'll learn _____ to  do  this, _ the Pep-per-mint Twist.

Well, 'round    and 'round,        up    and down,

'round and 'round,   up and down,  'round and 'round and   up and down,

one  two  three  kick,  one   two  three  jump.

Well, al - right __    all    night, __    well, al-right.
It's   o - kay _    all   day, __    it's   o-kay.

And you'll learn ____ to  do  this, _ the Pep-per-mint Twist.

Hey! _____                      Hey! _____

And you'll learn ____ to  do  this, _ the Pep-per-mint Twist!

## The Motown Sound

Motown is a **style** of rock music. **Listen** to Martha Reeves and the Vandellas sing the motown hit *Dancing in the Street.*

Motown groups perform special dance moves as they sing. How would you **move** to this song?

**Style** is the special sound that is created when music elements, such as rhythm and timbre, are combined.

8–17

### Dancing in the Street

**by Marvin Gaye, William Stevenson, and Ivy Hunter**

Motown is named after its hometown, Detroit. Detroit is known as the Motor City because of the many car factories there.

## Latin Roots

Many rock bands mix other music styles into their songs. **Listen** to Santana's version of *Oye como va*. It combines rock and roll and *salsa*.

**8–18**
**Oye como va**

**by Tito Puente
as performed by Santana**

The electric guitar is the featured solo instrument played by Carlos Santana.

### M·U·S·I·C · M·A·K·E·R·S
## Carlos Santana

**Carlos Santana** (born 1947) started playing guitar professionally when he was 13 years old. He has been the leader of the band Santana since the late 1960s. He won nine Grammy Awards in the year 2000.

## Poetry on the Move

Poetry can take you on a journey too. Read this poem and imagine a world beyond your home.

With a partner, choose some classroom instruments and **create** an accompaniment to this poem. Draw a musical map to show how your music goes.

# Around the World

*by Susan Katz*

All of the world is waiting out there,
Cradled in layers of sky
the color of mountain-lake blue;
People and places, adventures and fun;
All around the world,
the world is waiting for you.

UNIT
8

# Home
## and
# Away

Take a journey around
our musical world and
discover how music is
enjoyed by children
everywhere.

# A Musical Journey

"All the Way Around the World" is a song about children on a boat journey. **Listen** for the many musical styles in the accompaniment. Then **sing** the song with your class.

## All the Way Around the World

8–19

*Words and Music by Katherine Dines*

VERSE

D
1. This boat's gon-na car-ry hap-pi-ness,
2. This boat's gon-na car-ry har-mo-ny,

A₇
hap-pi-ness,
har-mo-ny,

D
hap-pi-ness.
har-mo-ny.

D
This boat's gon-na car-ry hap-pi-ness,
This boat's gon-na car-ry har-mo-ny,

A₇ D
All the way a-round the world.

All the way a - round _ the world this
boat's gon - na fly with its sails un - furled,
to ev - 'ry boy and ev - 'ry girl, _____
All the way a - round the world.

3. This boat's gonna carry love and peace, . . .
   *Refrain*

4. This boat's gonna carry hope and strength, . . .
   *Refrain*

# Hello, Friends!

People around the world greet each other in different ways. How do you greet your friends?

**Sing** "Hello!" and discover new ways to say "hello."

**8–21**

## Hello!

*Words and Music by Laszlo Slomovits*

**REFRAIN**

Hel - lo, hel - lo, hel - lo, hi, hi, hi,

Hel - lo, hel - lo, hel - lo, hi!    *Fine*

**VERSE**

1. In France they say, "Bon-jour," "Bon-jour." *(Echo)*

In Chi-na they say, "Ni-hau," "Ni-hau." *(Echo)*

In Is-rael they say, "Sha-lom," "Sha-lom." *(Echo)*

## Greet with a Beat!

**Listen** to "Hello!" **Move** around the room to the beat. Each time you hear a new greeting, stop and greet a classmate in a different way.

G₇                                                                (Echo)

In South Af - ri-ca _ they say,   "Du-me-la,"   "Du-me-la."

G₇                                              C

Some-times we shake hands;   we wave   and we grin. _

D₇                          G                    D. C. al Fine

We pat each oth-er on the back; _ we say, "Hi!   How you been?" _

2.  In Mexico they say, "Buenos Días," "Buenos Días."
    In Russia they say, "Zdrastvooyti," "Zdrastvooyti."
    In Japan they say, "Konnichi Wa," "Konnichi Wa."
    In India they say, "Namaste," "Namaste." . . .
    *Refrain*

## Greetings from Russia

**Listen** to Igor Stravinsky talk about how he composed *Greeting Prelude*. Then listen to the music. Do you hear a song you know?

 8–23

### Interview and Greeting Prelude

**by Igor Stravinsky**

Stravinsky composed *Greeting Prelude* in 1955 to celebrate the 80th birthday of a good friend.

**M·U·S·I·C  M·A·K·E·R·S**

## *Igor Stravinsky*

**Igor Stravinsky** (1882–1971) was born in Russia. Some of his most famous music was for ballet. Later in his life he moved to Hollywood, California. In 1982 his picture was put on a 2¢ postage stamp.

## Greetings from Thailand

In the Thai language, if you say *sawatdee* one way, it means "hello." If you say it another way, it means "goodbye."

Follow the direction of the melody in *"Sawatdee tuh jah."* Point to each pitch as you **sing**.

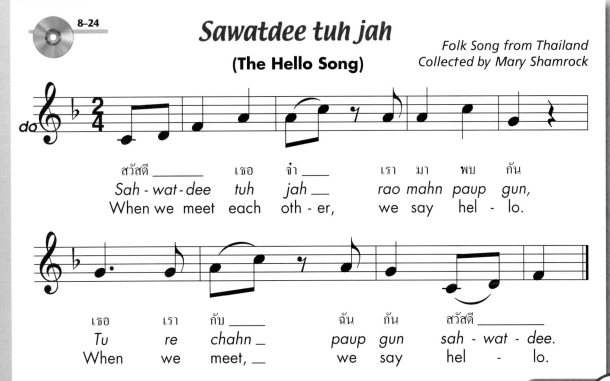

8–24

### Sawatdee tuh jah
**(The Hello Song)**

*Folk Song from Thailand*
*Collected by Mary Shamrock*

สวัสดี _____   เธอ   จ๋า ____   เรา   มา   พบ   กัน
*Sah - wat - dee   tuh   jah __   rao mahn paup   gun,*
When we meet   each   oth - er,   we   say   hel - lo.

เธอ   เรา   กับ _____   ฉัน   กัน   สวัสดี _____
*Tu   re   chahn __   paup gun   sah - wat - dee.*
When   we   meet, __   we   say   hel   -   lo.

# Follow the Leader

"Che che koolay" is a song from Ghana. It is in call-and-response form. A leader sings first, then everyone answers. Do the leader and the group sing the same melody?

258

# Rhythm Chat

With a partner, **create** a call-and-response game. **Clap** one of the "calls" below. Your partner can create a response. Then switch parts.

1.

2.

3.

People in Ghana sometimes use drums to send messages. ▶

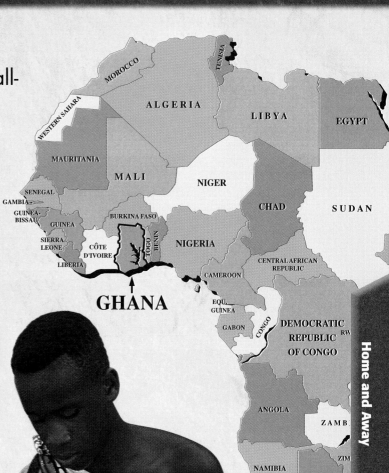

GHANA

Home and Away

# Do the Zudio!

People everywhere like to dance to music.
It is fun to dance to this song from the
United States.

## Zudio Moves

**Sing** the refrain of "Zudio."
Think of different ways you can
**move** to the beat.

# Zudio

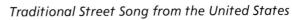

Traditional Street Song from the United States

REFRAIN

Here we go zu - di - o, zu - di - o, zu - di - o,

Here we go zu - di - o, all night long. __

Step back, Sal - ly, Sal - ly, Sal - ly,

Step back, Sal - ly, all night long. __

**VERSE**
Walkin' down the alley, what do I see?
I see a great big man from Tennessee.
Betcha five dollars I can catch that man,
Betcha five dollars I can catch that man.
To the side, to the side, to the side, side, side;
To the side, to the side, to the side, side, side,
Side, side, side.

My mama called the doctor; the doctor said,
    *(First time only)* "Oo, oh, I got a pain in my head."
    *(Second time only)* "Oo, oh, I got a pain in my tum."
    *(Third time only)* "Oo, oh, I got a pain in my side."
To the side, to the side, to the side, side, side;
To the side, to the side, to the side, side, side,
Side, side, side. *Refrain (First and second times only)*

# Singing Games HAWAIIAN STYLE

Children from near and far play singing games. *"Kapulu kane"* is a singing game from Hawaii.

**Sing** the song, and then play the game.

8–32

## Kapulu kane
### (Puili Game Song)

*Singing Game from Hawaii*

Ka - pu - lu,  pu - lu  Ka - ne,  Ka - pu - lu,  pu - lu  Ka - ne,

Ka - pu - lu,  pu - lu  Ka - ne  ku - ka - na - lu - a.

Ka - pu - lu,  pu - lu  Ka - ne,  Ka - pu - lu,  pu - lu  Ka - ne,

Ka - pu - lu,  pu - lu  Ka - ne  ku - ka - na - lu - a.

## Sticks Together

Children in Hawaii use *puili* [poo⌣EE-lee] sticks to make music and play games.

▲ *Puili* sticks are made of bamboo. The split ends make a special sound when they are tapped.

**Play** this *puili* stick game as you **sing** *"Kapulu kane."* Be sure to **tap** on each beat.

Tune In

Hawaii is the newest state in the United States. It is made up of 132 islands.

# CIRCLE

Children all over the world play circle games. **Sing** this circle game song from Brazil. Trace the melody as you sing.

**Move** to show where the phrases begin and end.

## CIRANDA
### (A Ring of Roses)

*Singing Game from Brazil*

Ci - ran - da      ci - ran - di - nha,
A      ring      a      ring      of      ro - ses,

Va - mos      to - dos      ci - ran - dar.
Let's      all      dance      a - round      to - day.

Va - mos      dar      a      me - ia      vol - ta,
Let's ___      dance      'round      in      a      cir - cle,

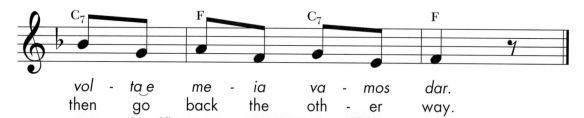

vol - ta e      me - ia      va - mos      dar.
then      go      back      the      oth - er      way.

## Do the Dance!

Form a circle to do the dance.
First skip around to the right.
Then skip around to the left.

### ✐Arts Connection

*Sally Walker* by Brenda
Joysmith (born 1953)
shows a popular African
American circle game. ▼

# Chinese Timbres

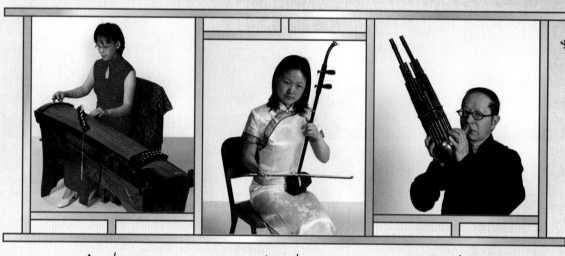

▲ zheng      ▲ erhu      ▲ sheng

**Listen** to this recording of instruments from China. Match the pictures of the instruments with the sounds you hear.

 **9–1**
**Chinese Instruments Montage**

 **Video Library** Watch *From Mao to Mozart: Isaac Stern in China*. See a Chinese student have a lesson on playing the *erhu*.

# A Game from China

**Sing** *"Diou shou juan'er."*
Which instruments sound familiar?

 9-2

# Diou shou juan'er

## (Hide the Scarf)

*English Words by David Eddleman*                    *Singing Game from China*

丟 ____ 手 ____ 絹          丟 ____ 手 ____ 絹
*Diou __ shou __ juan'er,*          *diou __ shou __ juan'er,*
Run the scarf a - round,          Where can it be found?

輕 輕 地 放 在 小 朋 友 的 後 ____ 面
*qing qing di fang xai xioa peng you di hou __ bian,*
Drop it be - hind some - one who's in the cir - cle;

大 家 不 要 告 訴 他
*Da jia bu yao gao su ta,*
When it's found you start the chase,

快 點 快 點 抓 住 他
*Kai dain'er, kai dain'er, zhua zhu ta.*
Catch her and you'll take her place.
(him) (his)

# Dancing Across the Ages

A long time ago, in France, the *pavane* and the *gaillarde* were popular dances. Imagine a big castle ballroom where royal subjects are dancing at an elegant party.

*Arts* Connection

▲ *Court Ball at the Palais du Louvre* (1582) Flemish School

# Ancient Dance Music

**Listen** to *Pavane et Gaillarde* and follow the listening map.
**Identify** where the meter changes in the music.

## Pavane et Gaillarde

**by Thoinot Arbeau**

The *pavane* [pah-VAHN] is a slow dance.
The *gaillarde* [gī-YAHRD] is a dance with jumps and kicks.

### *Pavane et Gaillarde* Listening Map

#### Pavane

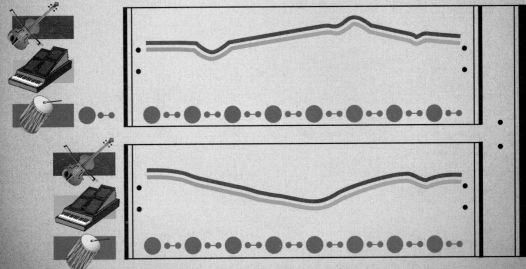

#### Gaillarde

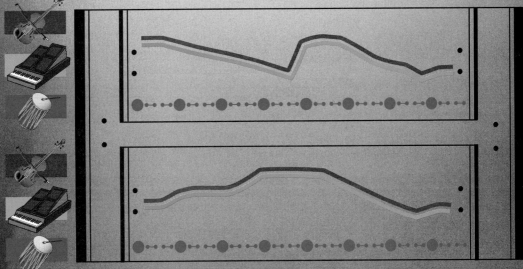

# Folk Dances

The polka started as a folk dance.
It later became a popular ballroom dance.

**Sing** *"Mon papa."* This French song is about
a girl who wants to dance the polka.

**9–7**

# Mon papa
### (My Papa)

*English Words by Edith Bicknell*                    *Folk Song from France*

do

G

1. Mon    pa - pa        ne    veut    pas
1. My     pa - pa        will   say    no,

D₇                          D          G

Que    je    dan - se,    que    je    dan - se,
No    more  danc - ing,   no    more  danc - ing,

G

Mon    pa - pa        ne    veut    pas
My     pa - pa        will   say    no,

D₇                                           G

Que    je    dan - se    la    pol - ka!
No    more  pol - ka    danc - ing    now!

2. Mais malgré sa défense,
   Moi je danse, moi je danse,
   Mais malgré sa défense,
   Moi je danse la polka!

2. Oh papa, dear papa,
   Let me go and dance the polka,
   Oh papa, dear papa,
   Let me dance the polka now!

# You Can Polka Too!

This is a dance you can do with your classmates.

9–11

 **Patty Cake Polka**

**Traditional Square Dance Tune**

The *Patty Cake Polka* has been danced in the United States for many years.

Play-

Imagine you are at a party in a big barn with decorations all around. The year is about 1870. Now **sing** and dance this play-party from the old days.

9–13

# Somebody Waiting

*Play-Party Song from the United States*

1. As I look in-to your eyes, I be-hold a glad sur-prise,

There is some-bod-y wait-ing for me.

2. There is some-bod-y wait-ing, there is some-bod-y wait-ing,

There is some-bod-y wait-ing for me.

3. Now choose two, leave the others, . . .   4. Swing the one, leave the other, . .

## Play-Party Clapping

**Clap** this rhythm with the song to help keep the play-party moving.

**Video Library** Watch *Folk Dance* to learn about other folk dances from around the world.

# A Maori Goodbye...

Maori [MOW-ree] people live in New Zealand. They often use hand movements to tell the stories of their songs.

"*Haere*" is a Maori goodbye song. **Perform** these body percussion rhythms with the song.

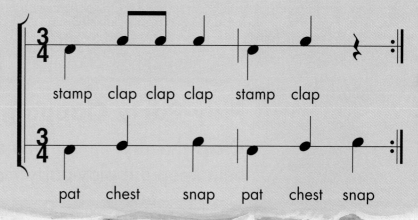

stamp   clap   clap   clap   stamp   clap

pat   chest   snap   pat   chest   snap

# Singing Goodbye

Now sing "Haere" with body percussion rhythms. What is the meter of the song?

9–17

# Haere
## (Farewell)

*English Words by David Eddleman*

*Maori Song from New Zealand*

Hae - re    hae - re    ra
Find    the    place    you    be - long,

kia    ka - ha    ki - a    to - a    e
Fare - well, ___ my    friend,    may    you    be    well.

ki    te    whe - nu - a    i    te    ta - ha
You    must    be    brave    and    you    must    be    strong,

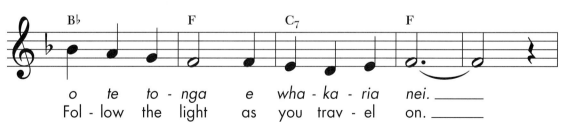

o    te    to - nga    e    wha - ka - ria    nei. _____
Fol - low    the    light    as    you    trav - el    on. _____

Hae - re    hae - re    hae - re    ra.
Fare - well,    fare - well,    my    friend, fare - well.

# Sing your Way Home

After a long trip, it is good to get home.

**Sing** this song about traveling home. **Describe** the form of the song.

9–21

# I'm Flying Home

*Words and Music by David Eddleman*

VERSE Eb       Eb/Bb      Bb

do

1. Fly - ing from an east - ern cit - y, ____
2. Fly - ing 'cross a snow - capped moun - tain, __

Eb       Eb/Bb   Bb

fly - ing to a west - ern town,
soar - ing 'cross a gras - sy plain,

Eb       Ab/Eb

I know an - y - place I'm head - ed,
North - west down to south - ern cli - mate,

Bb7       Eb     *Fine (after verse 4)*

I'm fly - ing home.

276

## Singing Well

As you **sing** the song, remember these two things. Sit up straight and keep your shoulders relaxed.

REFRAIN

Fly - ing, fly - ing, let me roam,

An - y - place I go is home.

3. Flying over thirsty desert,
   flying to New England's shore,
   Great Lakes to Southwest and onward,
   I'm flying home. *Refrain*

4. Flying from an eastern city,
   flying to a western town,
   I know anyplace I'm headed,
   I'm flying home. *Refrain*

# Walk with the Animals

Choose a favorite animal and **move** the way that animal does as you **sing** "What Do Animals Need?" See if your classmates can guess which animal you are!

## What Do Animals Need?

*Words and Music by the Banana Slug String Band*

**9–24**

**REFRAIN**

Em

*do*

1. What do an - i - mals need?    A wild home. __
2. What does ev - 'ry - one need?    A healthy home. __

What do an - i - mals need?
What does ev - 'ry - one need?
Room to roam. __

What do an - i - mals need?
What does ev - 'ry - one need?
Clean wa - ter and air. __

*To verses 1., 2., 3.*

What do an - i - mals need?
What does ev - 'ry - one need?
Love and care.

# Creature Feature

Animals are a very important part of our world. Here are some songs about caring for and enjoying the creatures of the land and sea.

# Talk with the Animals

Speak this rhythm. Then **play** it with "What Do Animals Need?"

Save    the Earth    and    ev'-ry-thing that's  in        it.

# Sing with the Animals

**Sing** the melody below. **Play** it on a xylophone.

Let's give    the crea-tures what they need.

# MUSIC MAKERS

## The Banana Slug String Band

**The Banana Slug String Band** entertains people with music while teaching them about science and ecology. The Slugs are "Airy" Larry Graff, Doug "Dirt" Greenfield, "Solar" Steve Van Zandt, and "Marine" Mark Nolan. They accompany their songs with guitars, mandolin, bass, harmonica, banjo, and percussion.

# FROG

**Listen** for different frog sounds in the song *"El coquí."* Can you create those sounds yourself?

 9–26

## EL COQUÍ
### (The Little Frog)

*English Words by José-Luis Orozco*

*Musical arrangement by José-Luis Orozco*
*Folk Song from Puerto Rico*

El  co - quí,  el  co - quí a mí me en - can - ta.
My  co - quí,  lit - tle  frog, how  I  love  you.

Es  bo - ni - to el  can - tar  del  co - quí.
For  your songs give  me  com - fort  and  peace.

Por  las  no - ches,  al  ir  a a - cos - tar - me
Ev - ery  night  I  can  go  to  sleep hap - py,

Me a dor - me - ce  can - tan - do  a - sí.
When I  hear  lull - a - bies  from  co - quí.

282

# MUSIC

## Hopping in Three

As you **listen** to "*El coquí*" again, **move** to show the meter.

### Tune In

Some frogs sing by squeezing air from their lungs. They keep their nostrils and mouth shut. This makes their vocal sacs puff out like a balloon.

**REFRAIN**

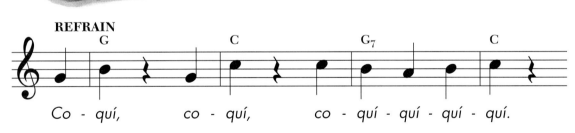

Co - quí,     co - quí,     co - quí - quí - quí - quí.

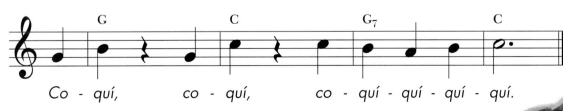

Co - quí,     co - quí,     co - quí - quí - quí - quí.

# Sounds of Nature

Nature creates wonderful music and art. What are some of your favorite sights and sounds in nature? **Sing** this song about wildlife by the waterside.

9–30

## Listen to the Water

*Words and Music by Bob Schneider*

REFRAIN

Lis - ten to the wa - ter, Lis - ten to the wa - ter

Roll - ing down ___ the riv - er. ___

Lis - ten to the wa - ter, Lis - ten to the wa - ter

Roll - ing down ___ the ri - ver. ___

## Natural Rhythms

Read these water wildlife names.
Match each name with its rhythm.

1. snake     a.

2. sandpiper     b.

3. snapping turtle     c.

**VERSE**

1.,2. Well, we saw some birds by the wa - ter - side, __
                   fish

We saw some birds by the wa - ter - side, __
                fish

We saw some birds by the wa - ter - side, __
                fish

Oh, oh, ___ by the wa - ter - side, _____

*D.C. al Fine*

Oh, oh, ___ by the wa - ter - side. __

3. . . . ducks . . .          4. . . . flowers . . .

# Creature Tale

*"Chawe chidyo chem'chero"* is a song story. There are many song stories from Africa. These stories are good for telling around a fire at night.

## The Story of the *Kudu*

**Listen** to this story about a *kudu* who wants to eat a family's garden.

**9–33**

## Chawe chidyo chem'chero

**Traditional story from Zimbabwe**

Learn how the *kudu* charms the family with his music and gets to eat all he wants.

### Tune In

A *kudu* is an antelope that lives in eastern and southern Africa. *Kudus* have grayish fur, and the male *kudu* has spiral horns.

## The *Kudu's* Song

**Sing** this song with the story.

 9–34

## Chawe chidyo chem'chero

*Shona Ngano Song from Zimbabwe*

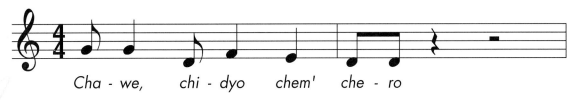

Cha - we,    chi - dyo   chem'   che - ro

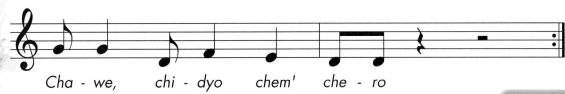

Cha - we,    chi - dyo   chem'   che - ro

## Play Along with the Song!

Now **play** this ostinato with the song.

low  high  high  high  low  high

Say and **play** this rhythm pattern with the song and story.

Don't eat    the gar - den    Ku - du.

## Perform the Story

**Perform** the story and take turns being the *kudu*. Who will play the other characters? What other animals could be part of the story?

**Sing** the *kudu's* song during the story. **Play** a drum or **clap** the rhythm you learned with the song.

Creature Feature

## Be a Cool Cat!

Now, use body percussion to **perform** this rhythm with *"Der sad to katte."*

Saa sa' den e - ne: "Hør min ven,"
Said one, "Now lis - ten here, my friend,"

krit - te - vit - te - vit - te - vit - te - vit bom bom,

"sku' vi ik - ke krav - le ned i - gen?"
"I ___ think we should get down a - gain,"

krit - te - vit - te - vit bom bom.

2. Og da de saa var kommet ned,
   krittevittevit bom bom.
   saa sa' den anden: "Hør min ven,"
   krittevittevit bom bom.
   "sku' vi ikke kravle op igen?"
   krittevittevittevittevit bom bom,
   og saa kravlede de op igen,
   krittevittevit bom bom.

2. They scrambled down and took a rest,
   krittevittevit bom bom.
   The other said, "No, up is best,"
   krittevittevit bom bom.
   So they climbed up that tree again,
   krittevittevittevittevit bom bom,
   And that's a game that has no end,
   krittevittevit bom bom.

# A Batty Melody

This folk song tells four creature tales.
Listen to "Leatherwing Bat."
Then move to act out the stories.

**Verse 1**
. . . heart's delight

**Verse 2**
. . . dressed in black

**Verse 3**
. . . head's been red

**Verse 4**
. . . as he flew

## Tune In

Bats use sound pulses to find things and to keep from crashing into them.

# Fly with the Melody

Now, **sing** the song and trace the direction of the melody. It takes the shape of a bat's flight pattern.

## Leatherwing Bat

*Folk Song from the British Isles*

1. "Hi," said the lit-tle lea-ther-wing bat, "I'll tell you the rea-son that,

The rea-son that I fly by night is be-cause I lost my heart's de-light."

**REFRAIN**

How-dy, dow-dy did-dle-o-day, How-dy, dow-dy did-dle-o-day,

How-dy, dow-dy did-dle-o-day, How-dy, dow-dy did-dle-o-day.

2. "Hi," said the blackbird,
   sitting on a chair,
   "Once I courted a lady fair;
   She proved fickle and turned her back,
   And ever since then
   I've dressed in black."
   *Refrain*

3. "Hi," said the woodpecker,
   sitting in the grass,
   "Once I courted a bonny lass;
   She proved fickle and from me fled,
   And ever since then
   my head's been red."
   *Refrain*

4. "Hi," said the greenfinch as he flew,
   "I loved one that proved untrue;
   And since she will no more be seen,
   Every spring I change to green."
   *Refrain*

# Rabbit Rhythms

**Sing** this song about a mother rabbit gathering food for her young.

 10–6

## Rabbit Footprints

*Words and Music by David Eddleman*

I spy rab - bit foot-prints in the snow,

She is gath - 'ring sup - per, I know,

To feed her lit - tle ones warm in the nest

Be - fore they set - tle down for a cold eve - ning

rest. _____ (hum) _____

## Rhythms to Play

**Play** these rhythm patterns with the song.

## Rabbit Thoughts

Read this poem by a twelve-year-old poet.
Then you can write your own rabbit poem.

### Rabbits

*by Noah Wager*

Rabbits come in many colors
caramel, black, and white.
They match the snow,
they match the clouds,
Their fur is clean and bright.

They jump, they skip, they run,
they hop on all four feet.
They gnaw on greens, carrots,
beans, and that is what they eat.

# Crabby Lullaby

Many children in Haiti know about crabs. They are all around the beaches and on their dinner tables! **Sing** this lullaby from Haiti, but don't worry. This crab won't really eat anyone's toes!

 10–8

## Deau-deau, ti pitit maman

### (Sleep, My Little One)

*English Words by Edith Bicknell*

*Lullaby from Haiti
as sung by Germaine Sorel*

Deau - deau, ti pi - tit ma - man.
Deau - deau, sleep my lit - tle one.

Deau - deau, ti pi - tit ma - man.
Deau - deau, sleep my lit - tle one.

Si ou pa Deau-deau, Crab la ap man - gé - ou. ___
Sleep now or, Deau-deau, Crab will eat your toes. _____

Si ou pa Deau-deau, Crab la ap man-gé - ou. ___
Sleep now or, Deau-deau, Crab will eat your toes. _____

# Join the Lullaby

**Play** the accompaniment below while others sing the song.

Metallophone

## *Arts* Connection

◀ *Untitled* by Audes Saul. Look at this painting by an artist from Haiti. Find the crab. What else do you see?

# A MUSICAL MENAGERIE

A menagerie [muh-NA-zher-ree] is a group of different animals. **Sing** this folk song from Kentucky about one person's menagerie.

10–12

## I Bought Me a Cat

*Folk Song from Kentucky*

C    G₇    C    G₇

1.,2.,3.,4.   I   bought   me   a   { cat, hen, duck, goose, }   and the   { cat hen duck goose }   pleased   me.

C    F    G₇    C

I   fed   my   { cat hen duck goose }   un - der   yon - der   tree.

298

# Animal Patterns

Practice these patterns. Decide which pattern sounds best for each animal. **Play** your pattern when the animal speaks in the song.

1.
F          G₇          C          Fine

Cat goes *fid - dle - i - fee!* _____

2. C          Repeat ending 1

Hen goes *chim-my-chuck, chim-my-chuck!*

3.          Repeat ending 2, then 1,
C          then proceed to verse 4

Duck goes *quack,    quack!*

4. C          Repeat 3, 2, 1

Goose goes *his - sy,  his - sy!*

# Worms at Work!

Worms don't often get much credit.
But the fact is, red worms can turn trash
into great soil for your garden! **Sing**
this song about respect for worms.

## Lots of Worms

*Words and Music by Patty Zeitlin*

1. Well, there are lots   of   worms __   way un - der the ground, __

Lots   of   worms ___   that I've nev-er   found. __   I'll bet they're

way   down   there ___   a - dig - gin' a - round, __

Way   un - der   the   ground. __

2. I dug the biggest hole I ever did dig,
   The biggest hole. It sure was big!
   And when I got to the bottom, you know what I found
   Way under the ground.

3. I found a worm to go on a fishing pole
   Down in the bottom of that deep, dark hole.
   But I left him alone 'cause he liked his home
   Way under the ground.

4. I found a bumpety bug with big black dots,
   Thirty-three legs and twenty-two spots.
   But I left it alone 'cause it liked its home
   Way under the ground.

5. I found an old sow bug curled up like a ball
   She didn't move from there at all.
   So I left her alone 'cause she liked her home
   Way under the ground.
   *Repeat verse 1*

# Wiggle Like a Worm!

If a worm took a break from work to dance, how many ways could it wiggle? **Listen** to *Disco Worm*. **Move** to show *legato* or *staccato* sounds in the music.

**10-15**
**Disco Worm**

**by Bryan Louiselle**
This disco dance tune was composed especially for a worm party!

## As the Worm Turns

Write a play about what happens after this worm meeting. Use your "worm moves" and the song "Lots of Worms" in your play.

## The Worms March

In your play, **perform** these ostinatos about ways worms help the planet.

For - ward     wig-gle for - ward     wig-gle

Gar-bage yum!     Gar-bage yum!

Aer-ate   the   soil,     clean up    the   Earth!

## It's Your Planet

You can help keep the Earth clean. One thing you can do is be sure to recycle whenever you can.

## Recycled Music

You can make music with stuff other people think is trash. **Listen** to *3+2* for some ideas. What do you think is making the sounds?

**10–16**
**3+2**

**by Donald Knaack**

*3+2* is from a collection of pieces written for and performed on recycled materials and everyday objects.

# Our
# Planet
# Earth

**The Earth is our home.
We must learn respect
for the many beauties
of our planet. We must
also keep Earth healthy.**

# Keep It Clean

Sing this song about some ways to keep Earth healthy.

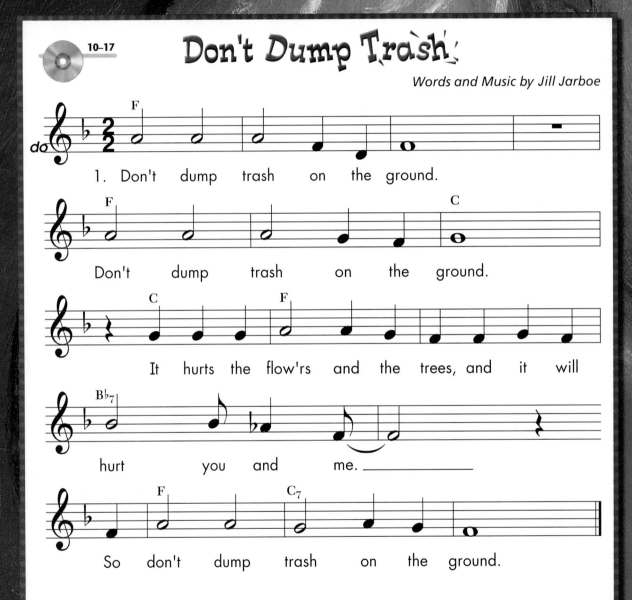

## Don't Dump Trash

10–17

*Words and Music by Jill Jarboe*

1. Don't dump trash on the ground.

Don't dump trash on the ground.

It hurts the flow'rs and the trees, and it will

hurt you and me. _____

So don't dump trash on the ground.

2. Don't dump trash in the sea.
   Don't dump trash in the sea.
   It hurts the fish and the whales
      from their fins down to their tails.
   So don't dump trash in the sea.

3. Don't dump trash in the air.
   Don't dump trash in the air.
   All the birds want to fly
      through a pretty clean sky.
   So don't dump trash in the air.

4. Don't dump trash on the moon.
   Don't dump trash on the moon.
   It fills the craters and the cracks
      on the front and on the back.
   So don't dump trash on the moon.

5. Don't dump trash anywhere.
   Don't dump trash anywhere.
   Except in the dump,
      where it's all in a lump.
   No, don't dump trash anywhere.

306

# Earth Sounds

Read aloud the poem "Breaks Free."
**Create** sounds to accompany the poem.

## Breaks Free

*by Frank Asch*

I just want to be
where the earth breaks free
of concrete and metal and glass,
of asphalt and plastic and gas,
where sun is king
and water is queen,
where cactus grows tall
and the air is clean.
I just want to be
where the earth breaks free
of fences and alleys and walls,
of factories and traffic and malls,
where owls sleep
in the heart of day
waiting for sunset
to hunt their prey,
where mountains rise
in seas of sand
and coyotes roam
across the land.

# A New Day

Each day gives us a new opportunity to care for and enjoy our planet. Music is a great way to start each day.

**Sing** this good morning song!

10–19

## Every Morning When I Wake Up

*Words and Music by Avon Gillespie*

Ev - e - ry morn - ing when I wake _ up

I have a new song to sing, my chil - dren,

Ev - e - ry morn - ing when I wake _ up

I have a new song to sing.

## Morning Music

**Play** these ostinatos to accompany "Every Morning When I Wake Up."

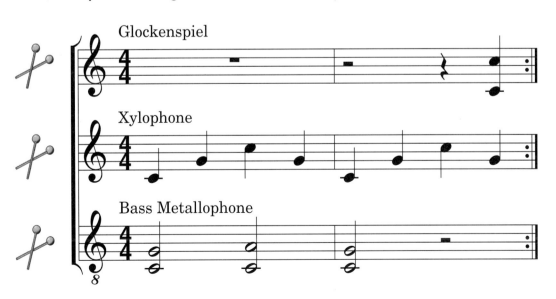

# Sing for the Trees

We need trees. The red cedar tree is very important to the Lummi people of Washington State. It is used for carving the great totem poles.

**Sing** this song about the cedar tree. On the last note of the song, sing softer and softer.

10–21

## Tall Cedar Tree

*Words and Music by Joseph Hillaire, Lummi Elder*
*As sung by Pauline Hillaire*

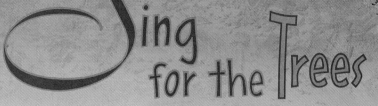

Tall _____ ce - dar tree,

1. clap your hands and sing to me. _____
2. clap your hands and dance with me. _____
3. clap your hands and play with me. _____

Wey he yoh, wey he he yoh,

wey he yoh ___ wey he he yoh. ___

# Song for the Earth

**Listen** to this Navajo song about the importance of rain for all living things.

### 10–23
## The Rain Song
**by Sharon Burch**

This song was written during a drought in 1988.

## MUSIC MAKERS

### Sharon Burch

**Sharon Burch** (born 1959) is a Grammy Award-winning singer and songwriter. Her mother is Navajo and her father is German. She says, "Having a German father and a Native mother helped me understand that a human can relate to all people . . . The whole planet is ours; there should be no boundaries."

# Music of the

The wind swirls all over the planet. It creates the energy that makes sailboats sail, kites fly, and windmills turn, but we cannot see it. How do we know it's there?

**Sing** this song about how the wind moves through trees.

 10–24

## Who Has Seen the Wind?

Words by Christina Rossetti

Melody from Zion's Harp

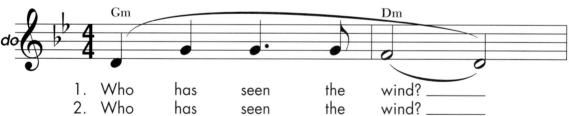

1. Who has seen the wind? _____
2. Who has seen the wind? _____

Nei - ther I nor _____ you!
Nei - ther you nor _____ I:

# Wind

## Move Like the Wind

Find the phrases in "Who Has Seen the Wind?"
**Move** to show each phrase as you **sing** the song.
Stretch your arms in wide curves and feel the wind.

But when the leaves hang trem - bling
But when the trees bow down — their heads

The wind is pass - ing through,
The wind is pass - ing by.

The wind is pass - ing ___ through.
The wind is pass - ing ___ by.

# Wind in Music

**Listen** to *Epilogue*, music about the cold wind of the Antarctic. Close your eyes and imagine the wind howling.

**10–25**
**Epilogue**

**from *Sinfonia Antarctica***
**by Ralph Vaughan Williams**

The wind sounds in this piece were created by a special device called a wind machine.

## To a Red Kite

*by Lilian Moore*

Fling
yourself
upon the sky.

Take the string
you need.
Ride high,

high
above the park.
Tug and buck
and lark
with the wind.

Touch a cloud,
red kite.
Follow the wild geese
in their flight.

**Tune In**

Ben Franklin discovered electricity while flying a kite.

314

# Fun with the Wind!

Flying kites in the wind is fun. Pretend your hand is a kite. Let your "kite hand" lead you.

## Let's Go Fly a Kite

*Words and Music by Richard M. Sherman and Robert B. Sherman*

Let's go fly a kite Up to the high - est height!

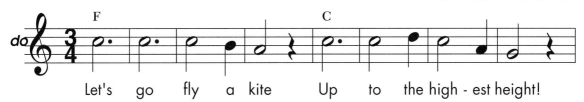

Let's go fly a kite And send it soar - ing

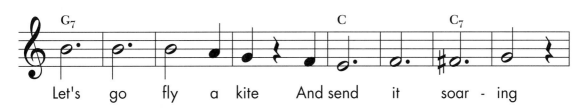

Up through the at - mos-phere, Up where the air is clear.

Oh, let's go ____ fly a kite! ____

**CD-ROM** Use *Making Music* software to create some "wind" music. Experiment with high and low sounds.

# Move with the Rain

Water is something our planet cannot live without. Rain is one way we get water. **Sing** this song about fun things to do on a rainy day. **Sing** *staccato* on the words *drip, drop.*

10–28

## Falling Rain

Words by Susan Marcus

Music by April Kassirer

**REFRAIN**

I can hear the fall - ing rain,

Think I'm gon - na stay in - side to - day,

Think I'm gon - na stay in - side and play and

*To Coda after verse 3*

lis - ten to the fall - ing rain.

## After the Rain

What happens to rain after it falls to the Earth? **Move** to show rain falling from clouds, flowing back to the oceans, then evaporating to become clouds and rain again.

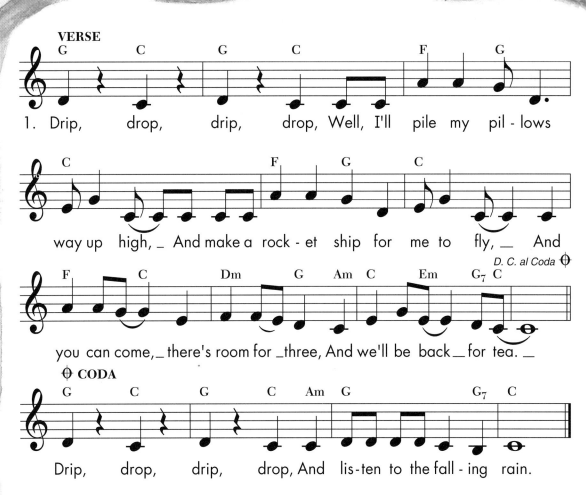

**VERSE**

1. Drip, drop, drip, drop, Well, I'll pile my pil-lows way up high, _ And make a rock-et ship for me to fly, _ And

*D. C. al Coda*

you can come, _ there's room for _ three, And we'll be back _ for tea. _

**CODA**

Drip, drop, drip, drop, And lis-ten to the fall-ing rain.

2. Drip, drop, drip, drop,
   A box will be my TV screen,
   I'll be a monster with my face all green,
   And in a monster voice you'll hear
      me say,
   "Buy monster's soup today." *Refrain*

3. Drip, drop, drip, drop,
   I'll fill my bathtub to the brim,
   And when it's full I'll climb right in,
   I'll keep my clothes on just in case
   I have to go someplace.
   *Refrain and Coda*

# Dance a Wonderful Day!

Plants, animals, and people need the sun to live. The sun warms and lights our planet. Think of a bright, sunny day. **Move** to show how it makes you feel.

 10–31

## Zip-a-Dee-Doo-Dah

Words by Ray Gilbert

Music by Allie Wrubel

Zip - a-dee-doo - dah, zip - a-dee - ay, ___

my, oh my, ___ what a won - der - ful day! ___

Plen - ty of sun - shine, head - in' my way, ___

Zip - a-dee-doo - dah, zip - a-dee - ay! ___

# Zip-a-Dee-Dance!

Skip around the room as you **sing** the Ⓐ section of "Zip-a-Dee-Doo-Dah." During the Ⓑ section, stand still and only move your arms.

Mis - ter Blue - bird on my shoul - der, ____

it's the truth    it's "act-ch'll,"    ev-'ry-thing is "sat-is-fact-ch'll."

Zip - a-dee - doo - dah,    zip - a-dee - ay! __

Won - der-ful feel - ing,    won-der-ful day. __

Sometimes, after it rains, you can see something special in the sky. It is very colorful. What is it?

**Sing** this song about a rainbow.

 10–33

# The Rainbow

*Children's Song from the United States*

1. Af - ter the rain is the rain - bow,

Af - ter the rain, then the sun comes out a - gain;

Af - ter the rain is the rain - bow,

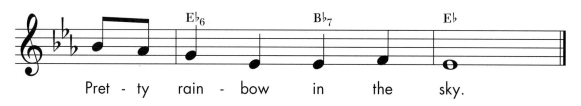

Pret - ty rain - bow in the sky.

2. Red, yellow, blue is the rainbow,
   Orange and green
    and a lovely violet;
   Painting the sky is the rainbow,
   Pretty rainbow in the sky.

3. Rainbows are telling a story,
   Rainbows are saying
    the sun comes out again;
   After the rain is the rainbow,
   Pretty rainbow in the sky.

# Rainbow Phrases

**Sing** this phrase.

*do*

Where do you find this phrase in "The Rainbow"? **Create** a movement for it. Each time you sing the phrase, **perform** your movement.

# A Louisiana Rainbow

**Listen** to this Cajun-style song from Louisiana.

 11–1
**L'arc en ciel**

**by Sharon Arms Doucet**

In English, the French title *L'arc en ciel* means "the arch in the sky." What do you think the song is about?

# Play into the Sunset

At the end of the day, you can watch a beautiful sunset. As the light fades into a night sky, what do you see?

**Play** one of these rhythm patterns as you **listen** to *"En nuestra Tierra tan linda."*

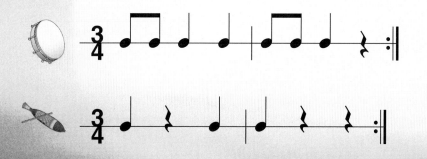

### Arts Connection

*Sunsets* (1956) by Diego Rivera. He painted twenty sunsets in Acapulco, Mexico. ▶

# Sky Sounds

Now **sing** this song about the beauty
of our planet Earth.

11–2

## En nuestra Tierra tan linda

*Words and Music by José-Luis Orozco*

1. En nues - tra Tie - rra tan lin - da _____
pron - to va a sa - lir el sol, _____
pron - to va a sa - lir el sol _____
en nues - tra Tie - rra tan lin - da. _____

2. En nuestra Tierra tan linda
pronto va a salir la luna,
pronto va a salir la luna
en nuestra Tierra tan linda.

3. En nuestra Tierra tan linda
pronto brillará una estrella,
pronto brillará una estrella
en nuestra Tierra tan linda.

# Star Textures

Have you ever made a wish upon a star? What did you wish for?

The Star Festival is a special day in Japan. Children make wishes and tie them to a tree branch. They believe that the stars will grant their wishes and help them improve their writing skills.

**11–5**

# Tanabata – sama
## (Star Festival)

*Words by Hanayo Gondo with Ryuha Hayashi*
*English Words by Mary Shamrock*

*Music by Kan-ichi Shimofusa*
*School Song from Japan*

1. さ　さ　の　は　さ　ら　さ　ら
1. Sa - sa　no　ha　sa - ra　sa - ra,
1. In　the　sky　the　stars　twin - kle　bright;

の　き　ば　に　ゆ　れ　る
No - ki - ba　ni　yu - re - ru,
Bam - boo　rust - ling　in　the　night.

## Starry Sounds

**Play** these patterns with *"Tanabata-sama"* as the class sings the song. **Describe** the texture. Is it thin or thick?

| | | | | | | | |
|---|---|---|---|---|---|---|---|
| お | ほ | し | さ | ま | き | ら | きら |
| O - | ho - | shi | sa - | ma | ki - | ra | ki - ra |
| Glit - | ter - | ing | sparks | of | sil - | ver | and gold |

| | | | | | | |
|---|---|---|---|---|---|---|
| き | ん | ぎ | ん | す | な | ご |
| Ki - | n | gi - | n | su - | na - | go. |
| High | a - | bove | us | we | be - | hold. |

2. *Goshiki no tanzaku,*
   *Watashi ga kaita,*
   *Ohoshi sama kira kira,*
   *Sora kara miteru.*

2. Choose your fondest wishes to write
   On the strips of paper bright.
   Then tie your wishes high on the tree;
   Stars will grant them, you will see.

*Amy Beach*

**Amy Beach** (1867–1944) was a child prodigy. She was composing and playing the piano when she was only four years old. Beach grew up to become the best-known American woman composer of her time. She played the piano for concerts in the United States and Europe. Her music was played by some of the most famous orchestras in the world.

## Star Gazing

**Listen** to the changing textures in *Sous les étoiles* as you follow the listening map.

11-9

## Sous les étoiles

from *Les Rêves de Columbine*, Op. 65 by Amy Beach

*Sous les étoiles* means "under the stars" in French.

# Sous les étoiles **Listening Map**

# Music for a Comet

*Halley Came to Jackson* is the story of someone who was alive for two visits by Halley's comet.

## Tune In

Halley's comet appeared in 1910, then again in 1986. How many years were in between appearances?

**Listen** to the song and learn when the comet visited. What instruments do you hear on the recording?

11–10
**Halley Came to Jackson**
by **Mary Chapin Carpenter**
Carpenter was inspired to write this song after reading the story by Eudora Welty.

## MUSIC MAKERS

### Mary Chapin Carpenter

**Mary Chapin Carpenter** (born 1958) is a singer-songwriter from Princeton, New Jersey. She has won many awards for her songs and recordings. She is active in organizations that are committed to making a better world for everyone.

# Care for the Ocean

**Sing** this song about the danger of littering in our oceans. **Describe** the form of the song.

## From Sea to Shining Sea

*Words and Music by Gene Grier and Lowell Everson*

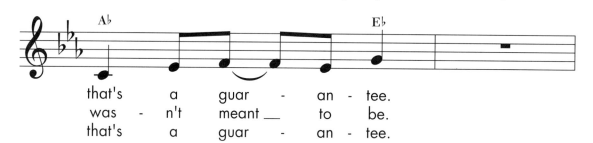

VERSE

E♭

1. Oil and wa - ter, they just don't mix;
2. Su - per tank - er crashed on a reef;
3. Oil and wa - ter, they just don't mix;

A♭                                E♭

that's a guar - an - tee.
was - n't meant __ to be.
that's a guar - an - tee.

E♭

Fish and wild - life get ver - y sick
Beach - es cov - ered with oil and grease
Fish and wild - life get ver - y sick

*3rd time to Coda* ⊕

A♭

from sea to shin - ing sea.
from sea to shin - ing sea.
from sea to shin - ing sea.

## Save the Sea Creatures

If we are careful to keep the waters clean, our fishy friends will survive.

**Create** more verses about keeping the oceans clean. **Sing** your new verses.

REFRAIN

From sea to shin - ing sea,

on this we will ___ a - gree.

To keep the wa - ter free

from ref - use and ___ de - bris.

*Coda*

From sea to shin - ing sea, from sea to shin - ing sea.

## Sing a Story

**Sing** this song about the stories you can find in music.

**11–13**

*Words and Music by Jill Gallina*

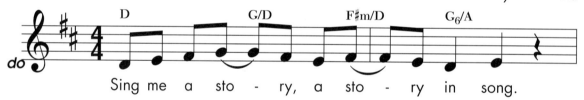

Sing me a sto - ry, a sto - ry in song.

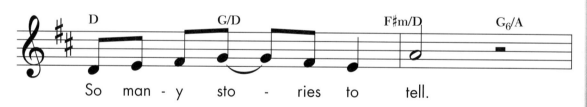

So man - y sto - ries to tell.

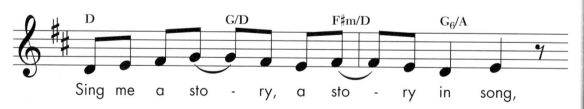

Sing me a sto - ry, a sto - ry in song,

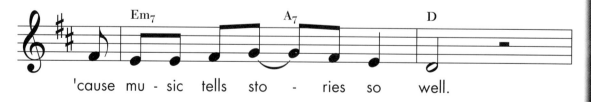

'cause mu - sic tells sto - ries so well.

# Perform a Story

**Music can tell stories in many ways.**

Sto - ries with fea - tures of ma - gi - cal crea - tures,

or jour - neys that take __ us a - long. __

Tall tales, or small _ tales, but the best of all __ tales,

are tales that are told __ with a song.

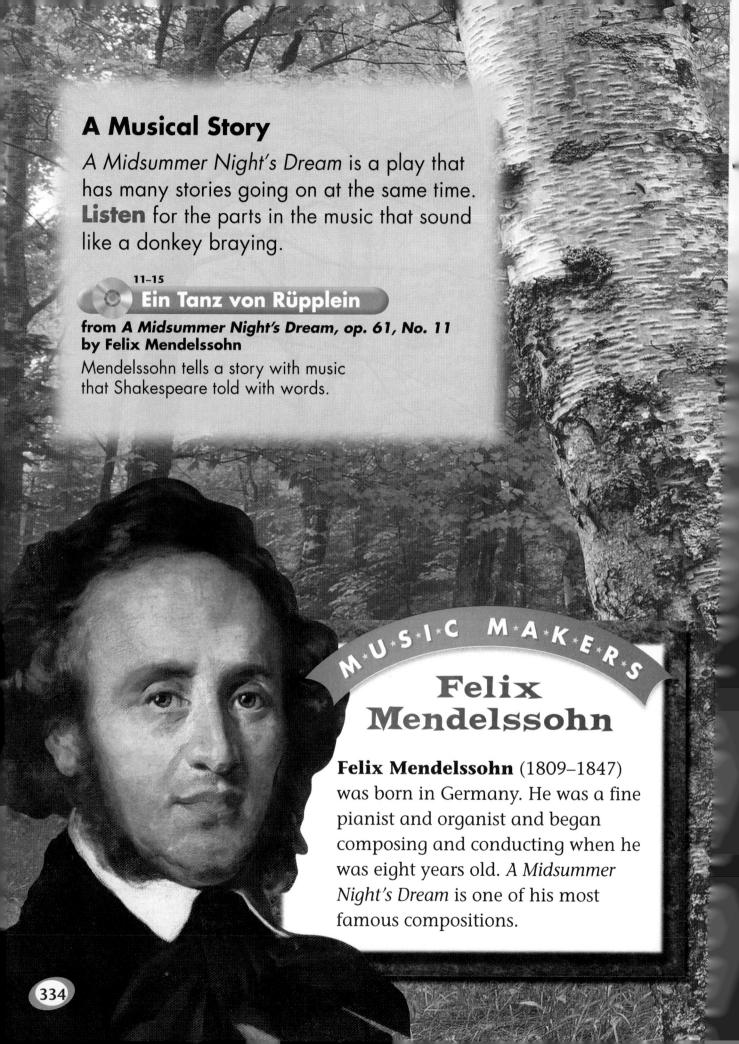

## A Musical Story

*A Midsummer Night's Dream* is a play that has many stories going on at the same time. **Listen** for the parts in the music that sound like a donkey braying.

11–15

**Ein Tanz von Rüpplein**

from *A Midsummer Night's Dream, op. 61, No. 11*
by **Felix Mendelssohn**

Mendelssohn tells a story with music that Shakespeare told with words.

### MUSIC MAKERS

## Felix Mendelssohn

**Felix Mendelssohn** (1809–1847) was born in Germany. He was a fine pianist and organist and began composing and conducting when he was eight years old. *A Midsummer Night's Dream* is one of his most famous compositions.

# Ein Tanz von Rüpplein

## Listening Map

# Sing a Dragon Tale

**Sing** this song that tells the story of Puff, the magic dragon, and his friend. What is the form of the song?

11–16

## Puff, the Magic Dragon

*Words and Music by Peter Yarrow and Leonard Lipton*

**VERSE**

1. Puff, the magic dragon,
     lived by the sea
   And frolicked in the autumn mist
     in a land called Honahlee.
   Little Jackie Paper
     loved that rascal Puff
   And brought him strings and sealing wax
     and other fancy stuff. Oh!
   *Refrain*

2. Together they would travel
     on a boat with billowed sail;
   Jackie kept a lookout perched
     on Puff's gigantic tail.
   Noble kings and princes
     would bow whene'er they came;
   Pirate ships would low'r their flag
     when Puff roared out his name. Oh!
   *Refrain*

3. A dragon lives forever
     but not so little boys;
   Painted wings and giant rings
     make way for other toys.
   One grey night it happened,
     Jackie Paper came no more,
   and Puff that mighty dragon,
     he ceased his fearless roar.
   *To Verse 4*

4. His head was bent in sorrow;
     green scales fell like rain.
   Puff no longer went to play
     along the cherry lane.
   Without his lifelong friend,
     Puff could not be brave,
   so Puff that mighty dragon
     sadly slipped into his cave. Oh!
   *Refrain*

# Jabuti's Song SAVES THE DAY

Kibungo is the meanest, scariest beast of the Amazon rain forest. **Listen** to the story and follow along with the pictures.

11–18
**Kibungo, Beast of the Forest**

Now you can **perform** the Kibungo story with your class.

# Songs for a Story

**Sing** these songs that go with the story of *Kibungo, Beast of the Forest.*

The first song is Kibungo's theme song.

**11–19**

## KIBUNGO

*Story-Song from the Amazon Rainforest*

Ki - bun - go    o - i    bi - cho do ma - to.
Ki - bun - go, oh - oh,    beast of the for - est.

Ki - bun - go    o - i    bi - cho do ma - to.
Ki - bun - go, oh - oh,    beast of the for - est.

Jabuti uses this song to trick Kibungo.
**Move** to show the form of the song.

11–23

# O PIÃO ENTROU
## (The Top Joined the Circle)

*English Words by C. P. Language Institute*                                    *Game Song from Brazil*

VERSE

O    pi - ão    en - trou    na    ro - da ó    pi - ão
Oh,   the   top   joined   in    the    cir - cle    to   spin.

O    pi - ão    en - trou    na    ro - da ó    pi - ão,
Oh,   the   top   joined   in    the    cir - cle    to   spin.

REFRAIN

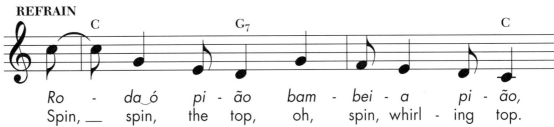

Ro  -  da ó    pi - ão    bam - bei - a    pi - ão,
Spin, __   spin,    the    top,    oh,    spin,   whirl - ing   top.

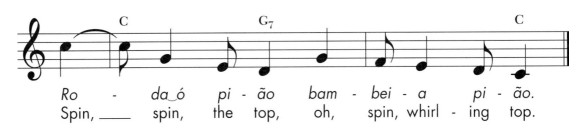

Ro  -  da ó    pi - ão    bam - bei - a    pi - ão.
Spin, __   spin,    the    top,    oh,    spin,   whirl - ing   top.

2.  *Sapateia no terreiro*
      *ó pião,* (Repeat)
    Refrain

3.  *Pega a mão do teo parceiro*
      *ó pião,* (Repeat)
    Refrain

2.  Tap away in the clearing,
      dance, spinning top. *(Repeat)*
    *Refrain*

3.  Take your partner by the hand,
      spinning top. *(Repeat)*
    *Refrain*

Perform a Story

# Sing a Legend

Sometimes people use songs to tell a story about their beliefs. Sing this song from the Pima people of Arizona. It tells how they believe Earth began. Move to show the direction of the melody.

## Chuhwuht

11–29

*Native American Song of the Pima
as sung by Chief Visak-Vo-o-yim*

Chuh - wuht - tah ma - ka - i, chuh - wuht - tuh na - to.

Chuh-wuht - tuh ma - ka - i, chuh - wuht - tuh na - to.

Hi - ma - lo, hi - ma - lo,

Hi - ma - lo, hi - ma - cho!

## Story in a Poem

Songs and poems tell stories in their own ways. This poem is from the Wintu people of California. It is part of their story about the beginning of the world.

# The Stars Streaming in the Sky

*Traditional Wintu*

The stars streaming in
the sky are my hair.
The round rim of the
Earth which you see
Binds my starry hair.

# SOUNDS OF A TRAIN

Before airplanes were invented, trains were the speediest form of travel.

**Listen** to the accompaniment of this railroad song. **Describe** the sounds you hear.

11–32

## She'll Be Comin' 'Round the Mountain

*Railroad Song*

1. She'll be com - in' round the moun - tain when she
2. She'll be driv - in' six white hor - ses when she

comes, (toot, toot!) She'll be com - in' round the moun-tain when she
comes, (chug, chug!) She'll be driv - in' six white hor - ses when she

comes, (toot, toot!) She'll be com - in' round the
comes, (chug, chug!) She'll be driv - in' six white

344

# Creating Train Sounds

**Create** your own special sound effects to accompany the song. Make them sound like a train.

moun - tain, She'll be com - in' round the moun - tain, She'll be
hor - ses, She'll be driv - in' six white hor - ses, She'll be

com - in' round the moun - tain when she comes. (toot,    toot!)
driv - in'  six white hor - ses when she comes. (chug,    chug!)

3.  Oh, we'll all have chicken and dumplings when she comes, (yum, yum!) . . .

4.  Oh, we'll all go out to meet her when she comes, (Hi, there!) . . .

# A Song that Grows!

**Create** movements to help you remember the verses of this song. A song that keeps growing is called a **cumulative song.** Do you know other songs like this?

A **cumulative song** gets longer as each new verse is added.

## The Tree in the Wood

*Traditional Cumulative Song from England*

1. All in ___ a ___ wood there grew a tree,
2. Now on ___ this ___ tree there grew a limb,

The fi - nest ___ tree you ev - er did see.
The fi - nest ___ limb you ev - er did see.

*Repeat as necessary*

The tree was in the ground,
The limb was on the tree,

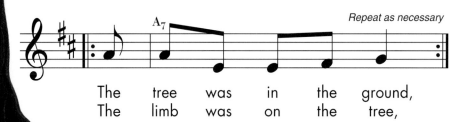

# Tell Your Own Story

Write a cumulative story with a partner.
Then **create** sound effects to accompany
your story.

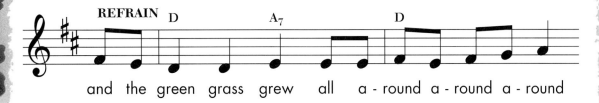

REFRAIN

and the green grass grew all a-round a-round a-round

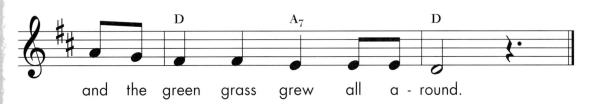

and the green grass grew all a-round.

3. Now on this limb there grew a branch,
   The finest branch you ever did see.
   The branch was on the limb,
   The limb was on the tree,
   The tree was in the ground,
   *Refrain*

4. Now on this branch there was a bough, . . . *Refrain*

5. Now on this bough there was a twig, . . . *Refrain*

6. And on this twig there was a leaf, . . . *Refrain*

7. And by this leaf there was a nest, . . . *Refrain*

8. And in this nest there was an egg, . . . *Refrain*

9. And in this egg there was a bird, . . . *Refrain*

10. And on this bird there was a wing, . . . *Refrain*

11. And on this wing there was a feather, . . . *Refrain*

12. And on this feather there was a flea, . . . *Refrain*

# Sing a Funny Story

Music and poetry often tell stories just for fun. **Sing** the story of "The Crocodile." Then read the poem.

12–3

## The Crocodile

*Traditional*

She   sailed   a - way   on   a   love - ly   sum - mer   day

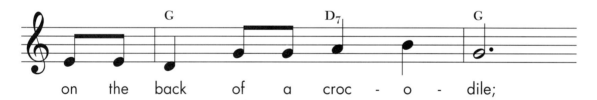

on   the   back   of   a   croc - o - dile;

"You'll   see,"   said   she,   "he's   as   tame   as   tame   can   be,

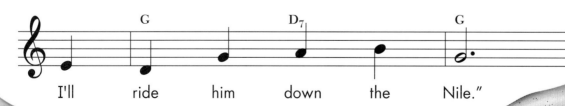

I'll   ride   him   down   the   Nile."

## How Doth the Little Crocodile
*by Lewis Carroll*

How doth the little crocodile
Improve his shining tail,
And pour the waters of the Nile
On every golden scale!
How cheerfully he seems to grin,
How neatly spreads his claws,
And welcomes little fishes in
With gently smiling jaws!

## Melody Patterns

Find repeated patterns in the melody of "The Crocodile."

Perform a Story

The croc winked his eye as she bade them all good-bye,

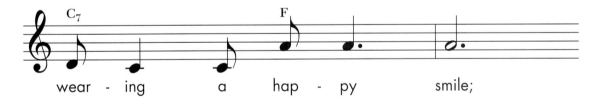

wear - ing     a     hap - py     smile;

At the end of the ride the lad - y was in - side

and the smile was on the croc - o - dile! Yum Yum!

# Cajun Crocodile Song

The Cajuns are people in Louisiana whose ancestors were French. Here is a Cajun song about two crocodiles. **Listen** for the same and different phrases in the song.

12–4

## Deux cocodries
### (Two Crocodiles)

*English Words by Edith Bicknell*                    *Cajun Singing Game from Louisiana*

Deux     co - co - dries     sont  al - lés   à    la   guer - re,
Two     croc - o - diles     were  go - ing   off   to   war, ___

dis - ant   "a - dieu"    à   leurs  pe - tits   en - fants. ___
Say - ing   "so long!"    as   they  went  out   the   door. ___

Leurs    lon - gues queues   traîn - aient dans  la    pous-sièr - e,
Long     tails  be - hind,   through mud they  did   ad - vance, ___

ils     sont  al - lés    com - battre les   é - lé - phants. _
Ea - ger   to  fight    their foes  the   el - e - phants. _

**F**

Si     les   co - co - dries, les   co - co - dries, les   co - co - dries ___
If     the  croc - o - diles, the  croc - o - diles, the  croc - o - diles ___

**C₇**                                                                              **F**

sur   le  bord d'ba-you  se  sont per - dus, n'en par-lons   plus, ___
lose their way   a - long the   ba - you, then  our  sto - ry's  through, _

**F**

Si     les   co - co - dries, les   co - co - dries, les   co - co - dries ___
If     the  croc - o - diles, the  croc - o - diles, the  croc - o - diles ___

**C₇**                                                                              **F**

sur   le  bord d'ba-you  se  sont per - dus, n'en par-lons   plus. ___
lose their way   a - long the   ba - you, then  our  sto - ry's  through. _

# Dancing Animals

You are invited to an animal dance! Which animal would you like to be? **Sing** the story "Jig Along Home."

12–8

## Jig Along Home

*Words and Music by Woody Guthrie*

VERSE

F                                                    C₇

1. I went to the dance and the an - i - mals came;
2. ⅞ Fishing worm __ danced the __ fish - ing __ reel;

C₇                                    F

The jay - bird danced with horse - shoes on.
⅞ Lob - ster danced on the pea - cock's tail.

F                                    B♭

The grass - hop - per danced till he fell on the floor!
⅞ Ba - boon __ danced with the ris - ing __ moon.

F            C₇            F

Jig a - long, jig a - long, jig a - long home.

# Your Own Dance Moves

Create your own movements for each animal.
How will you **move** during the refrain?

**REFRAIN**

Jig, jig - a jig, jig - a jig a - long home,

Jig, jig - a jig, jig - a jig a - long home.

Jig a - long, jig a - long, jig a - long home.

Jig, jig - a jig, jig - a jig a - long home.

3. Mama rat took off her hat,
   Shook the house with the old tom cat.
   The alligator beat his tail on the drum,
   Jig along, jig along, jig along home.
   *Refrain*

4. The boards did rattle and the house
      did shake;
   The clouds did laugh and the world
      did quake.
   New moon rattled some silver spoons,
   Jig along, jig along, jig along home.
   *Refrain*

5. The nails flew loose and the floors
      broke down;
   Everybody danced around and
      around.
   The house came down and the
      crowd went home,
   Jig along, jig along, jig along home.
   *Refrain*

# A Story with a Moral

**Listen** to a song that tells a famous story. What is the moral, or lesson, of the story?

**12–9**
## Yertle the Turtle

**by The Red Hot Chili Peppers**

This popular group wrote the song, *Yertle the Turtle*, based on the story by Dr. Seuss.

## Create Story Music

**Create** your own music to go with a story you like. Follow these steps.

1. Form a group of four or five people.
2. Choose a story.
3. Decide what instruments you want to use.

Remember, you can
- Create a rhythm.
- Invent a melody.
- Play an ostinato.

**Perform** your story and music for the class.

# A Climbing Song

Have you ever been the first in line? How did you get there? **Sing** this song about taking care of others as you climb the ladder of success.

12–10

*Words and Music by Bryan Louiselle*

C₇ ... F

You might be a ver - y good climb - er

D₇ ... Gm

But no mat - ter how high you go,

C ... A₇

Take the time, make the time

Dm ... G ... C

To look af - ter those be - low.

## Melody with Steps

**Sing** the song again. How does the melody climb upward?

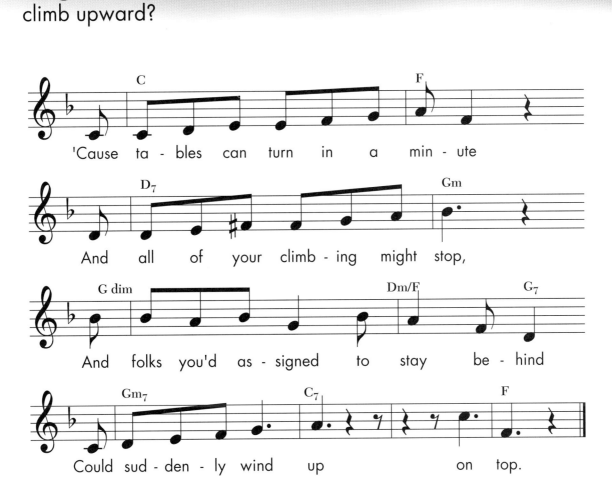

'Cause ta - bles can turn in a min - ute

And all of your climb - ing might stop,

And folks you'd as - signed to stay be - hind

Could sud - den - ly wind up on top.

## Sing to Celebrate

Here is a song you can **sing** for any special occasion.

It's a Celebration!

Words and Music by Katherine Dines

We are smil - ing in the sun

As the sea - sons go and come.

Fam - i - lies _____ a - round the world

Wel - come ev - 'ry boy and girl.

It's a cel - e - bra - tion, __ a cel - e - bra - tion,

It's a cel - e - bra - tion, __ a cel - e - bra - tion. __

# Celebrate the Season

**People around the world celebrate in many ways throughout the year. What special days do you celebrate with your family?**

# Fiesta Time!

Fiestas are big parties where people celebrate with singing and dancing. This song is written in a style called *huayno*. Let's go to the fiesta!

## Vamos a la fiesta

12–14

### (Let's Go to the Party)

*Words and Music by Juanita Newland-Ulloa*
*From Canta Conmigo, Vol. 2*

Va - mos a la fies - ta la fies - ta la fies - ta
Let's go to the par - ty, the par - ty, the par - ty

Va - mos a la fies - ta a go - zar
Let's go to the par - ty, we'll have fun.

To - dos los ni - ñi - tos muy chi - qui - ti - tos.
All the lit - tle chil - dren, they'll all be danc - ing.

To - dos los ni - ñi - tos a bai - lar.
All the lit - tle chil - dren, they will sing.

## Fiesta Percussion

**Play** these rhythm patterns to accompany
"*Vamos a la fiesta.*"

Now **improvise** your own rhythm patterns
while the class sings the song.

# OOOOooh! It's Halloween!

Here is a spooky song for Halloween. **Sing** "Skin and Bones." Use dynamics to express the mood of the song. How will you sing *BOO!* in the song?

  12–18

## Skin and Bones

*Folk Song from Kentucky*

1. There was an old wo-man all skin and bones,
2. She lived __ down by __ the old grave-yard,

Oo - oo - oo - ooh! __ 7. She op-ened the door and BOO!

3. One night she thought she'd take a walk, . . .

4. She walked down by the old graveyard, . . .

5. She saw the bones a-lyin' around, . . .

6. She went to the closet to get a broom, . . .

## A Halloween Chat

An owl and a pumpkin have a friendly chat in the song on the next page. Use your voice to show the two characters.

# The Owl and the Pumpkin

*Words by Betty Barlow and Victoria Shima*

*Music by Betty Barlow*

An owl in the tree looked down be-low and winked his eye.

"Who are you? Who are you?"

A pump-kin on the ground looked up and gave a friend-ly shout:

"Yoo - hoo! Yoo - hoo!"

The full moon said that they should get to - geth - er.

So now you'll hear in ev-'ry kind of weath - er:

"Who are yoo - hoo! Who are yoo - hoo!

Who are yoo - hoo!"

# Harvest Time

"Perot" is a song for the Jewish harvest holiday called *Sukkot*. As you **sing** the song, **move** to show the phrases.

12–22

## Perot
### (Fruit)

*English Words by David Eddleman*        *Traditional Song for Sukkot*

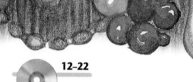

Pe - rot,        pe - rot!
Buy    fruit!    Buy    fruit!

Mi  ro - tzeh lik - not    Pe - rot  le - chag Suk - kot?
Who will  buy  my  fruit    to   ce - le - brate Suk - kot?

A - na - vim ve - ta - pu - chim,  a - na - vim ve - ta - pu - chim,
In  the  suk - kah you will dine, Grapes and ap - ples, oh,  so  fine;

Ve - ag - va - ni - yah    lit - lot  al  gag  Suk - kah.
Plump to - ma - toes, too,   are  hang - ing  there  for  you.

# A *Sukkot* Tradition

*Sukkot* is celebrated in the fall and lasts nine days. One of the traditions is to build a *sukkah*, or tent, by the house and decorate it with flowers, fruits, and vegetables.

Celebrate the Season

# Celebrate Thanksgiving

In the United States, many people celebrate Thanksgiving Day. Often people gather with friends and family for a holiday meal.

Here is a Thanksgiving song for you to **sing**.

12–26

## Thanksgiving Is Near

*Words and Music by Grace Nash*

1. Oc - to - ber is o - ver, Thanks-giv - ing is near.

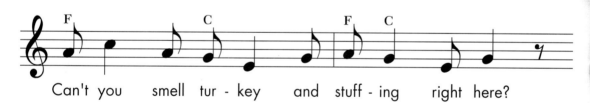

Can't you smell tur - key and stuff - ing right here?

And when it is o - ver and thanks have been said,

it won't be the tur - key but me stuffed in - stead!

2. The Thanksgiving table is loaded with treats.
   It's hard to use caution and not overeat.
   But when it is over and I'm stuffed in bed,
   I'll wish that the turkey had gobbled instead.

# A Thanksgiving Poem

Listen to this poem. Then **create** a rhythm pattern to accompany the poem.

## Setting the Thanksgiving Table
*by X. J. Kennedy*

Fetch bouquets of bittersweet.
Give them to wild birds to eat.

Bring the homely freckled gourd.
Let it ornament our board.

Bring the pumpkin plump in shape,
Bring the perfect purple grape.

Pile the polished apples high,
Granny Smith and Northern Spy,

Bring the chestnut in its fur
Coat of bristly brownish burr,

Bring in sun-bleached stalks, each ear
Ripe and golden as the year.

Bring, each day you wake and live,
Fresh supplies of thanks to give.

**LESSON 5**

Element: FORM | Skill: SINGING | Connection: SOCIAL STUDIES

# CHANUKAH
## The Festival of Lights

Chanukah is a Jewish holiday. It is usually celebrated in December. Every night for eight nights, a candle is lit in a special candleholder. This candleholder is called a *menorah*.

Here is a song you can **sing** to celebrate Chanukah.

### Chanukah Is Here!

12–28

*Words and Music by Judith Eisenstein and Frieda Prensky*

Flick - er lit - tle can - dles; flick - er bright for Cha - nu - kah.

Se - vi - von go spin - ning round and round on Cha - nu - kah.

Flick - er lit - tle can - dles, all eight nights of Cha - nu - kah.

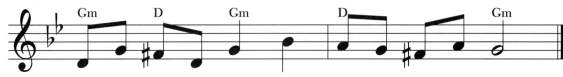

Se - vi - von go spin - ning, Cha - nu - kah is here!

## Another Chanukah Song

"Ner li" is another Chanukah song that you can sing. **Describe** the form of this song.

Latkes are one of the favorite foods eaten at Chanukah time. They are fried crispy potato pancakes.

12–30

### Ner li
### (The Light)

Words by Levin Kipnis
English Words by David ben Avraham

Music by Mifalei Tarbuth

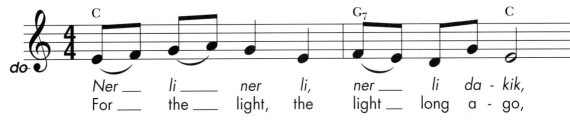

Ner __ li ____ ner li, ner __ li da - kik,
For __ the __ light, the light __ long a - go,

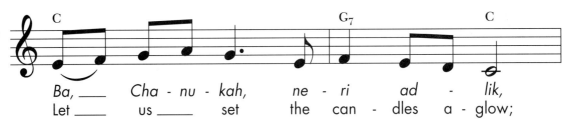

Ba, ____ Cha - nu - kah, ne - ri ad - lik,
Let ____ us ____ set the can - dles a - glow;

Ba, Cha - nu - kah, ne - ri a ir
Come, Cha - nu - kah, where light be - longs,

Ba, Cha - nu - kah, shir - im a - shir.
Come, Cha - nu - kah, we sing your __ songs.

Celebrate the Season

# Celebrate Christmas

Christmas is a holiday that celebrates the birth of Jesus. In the United States, Christmas is on December 25. Songs for Christmas are called *carols*. Here is a German Christmas carol you can **sing**.

 12–34

## O laufet, ihr Hirten

### (Come Running, You Shepherds)

*English Words by George K. Evans*          *Traditional Silesian Carol from Germany*

O  lau - fet  ihr  Hir - ten,  lauft  al  -  le  zu - gleich,
Come  run - ning,  you  shep - herds,  as  fast __ as  you  can,

Und  neh - men  Schal - mei - en  und  Pfeif - en  mit  euch!
With  flutes  and  with  bag - pipes,  and  with _ your  whole  clan.

Lauft _  al - le __ zu - mal  mit _ freu - di - gem __ Schall,
We're . go - ing _ to _ see,  In _ Beth - le - hem's _ stall,

Nach  Beth - le - hem  zum  Kripp - lein,  zum  Kripp - lein  im  Stall!
The  child _ whom  the  an - gels  an - nounced _ to  us  all.

## Santa Is Coming

The story of Santa Claus came to the United States with European immigrants.

**Listen** to this song about Santa Claus. Then **describe** the direction of the melody.

Words and Music by Elizabeth Gilpatrick

It's Santa – Again!

12–38

1. See the rein-deer tak-ing flight _____
2. Stashed be-hind him 'way in back _____

On a clear De-cem-ber night. _____
I see his e-nor-mous pack. _____

Can you see him flash-ing by,
I have heard it's filled with toys,

Out a-cross the win-ter sky?
For all the girls and all the boys.

You'll miss him if you blink your eye: it's San-ta a-gain!
Hush now, don't you make a noise: it's San-ta a-gain!

# Winter Fun!

Imagine taking a sleigh ride on a snowy night. What would you see? What kinds of sounds would you hear on a sleigh ride?

Here is a festive song you might **sing** on your sleigh ride.

12–40

## Jingle Bells

*Words and Music by James Pierpont*

**VERSE**

Dash-ing through the snow,    In a one-horse o - pen sleigh,

O'er the fields we go,    Laugh-ing all the way.

Bells on Bob - tail ring,    Mak-ing spir - its bright;    What

fun it is to ride and sing A sleigh-ing song to - night! Oh!

## *Arts* Connection

▲ *Holiday Sleigh Ride* (1993)
serigraph by Jane Wooster Scott

**REFRAIN**

Jin - gle bells,    jin - gle bells,    Jin - gle    all    the way!

Oh, what fun    it is    to ride In a one-horse o - pen    sleigh! _

Jin - gle bells,    jin - gle bells,    Jin - gle    all    the way!

Oh, what fun    it is    to ride In a one-horse o - pen sleigh!

# Going on a Sleigh Ride!

**Listen** to *Sleigh Ride*. Do you hear something that sounds like a cracking whip? What instrument sounds like a neighing horse at the end?

**12–42**
**Sleigh Ride**

**by Leroy Anderson**

Anderson uses sleigh bells and a slapstick to make this piece really sound like a sleigh ride.

## Leroy Anderson

**Leroy Anderson** (1908–1975) was born in Cambridge, Massachusetts. He composed orchestra music using unusual sounds, such as a typewriter, a ticking clock, and sandpaper.

## A Living Snowman?

**Listen** to *Frosty, the Snowman.* **Move** to show the changing moods in the song.

12–43

### Frosty, the Snowman

**by Jack Rollins and Steve Nelson**

In 1969 this song was the inspiration for a Christmas television special.

## Rap and Play

Did you ever make a snowman? This rap song tells you how.

13–1

# Mister Snow Rap

*Words by Linda Walsh*                    *Rhythmic Setting by Bob Demmert*

1. I take some snow from off the ground, __
2. I roll the ball back, to and fro, ___

And make a snow - ball, hard and round. __
By add - ing flakes, I watch it grow. __

3. Repeat three times
   and stack them high,
   Then add a nose, a mouth, and eyes.

4. My job's complete
   and now I know
   That I've created Mister Snow.

**Play** these rhythm patterns with "Mister Snow Rap."

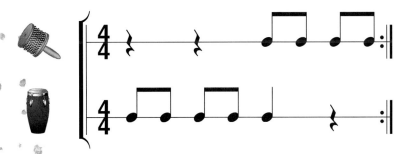

# CELEBRATE KWANZAA

*Kwanzaa* is an African American celebration.
It lasts for seven days.

**Sing** this song to learn about *Kwanzaa*.
**Move** to show the direction of the melody.

## A KWANZAA CAROL

*Words and Music by Reggie Royal*

VERSE

1. We sing of joy and glad-ness    a song of hope and peace.
2. For sev-en days we ga-ther,  rich prin-ci-ples  to  learn.

A *Kwan-zaa* ce - le - bra-tion  that means so much to    me.
We learn that we have val - ue    and share what we have earned.

From A - fri - ca    so long a - go    a  peo-ple came to   see,
We keep a strong com-mun - i - ty  when we stand up  and say:

That each one was  a  part of what I  was  to   be.
Each per-son  is  im - por-tant in their  way. _____

**REFRAIN**

F ... C7

Light the lights so bright, ce - le - brate,

F ... C ... F

for it's *Kwan-zaa* time. We will laugh and sing a

F ... B♭ ... C7 ... F

joy - ful song at *Kwan* - *zaa.*

# Living the Dream

Martin Luther King, Jr. was an important American leader. He dreamed of equality and justice for all people. He worked hard to help make these dreams come true.

**Perform** this rap to celebrate the life of Martin Luther King, Jr.

13–5

# A Kid Like Me

*Words and Music by Cathy Fink and Marcy Marxer*

There once was a preacher, Martin Luther King,
He worked day and night to hear freedom ring,
From Selma to Montgomery he led the people
In a struggle to create equal rights for all people.
He didn't use violence, no guns or knives.
His message was one that revered our lives.
We remember his speech, "I have a dream."
He did a lot for kids like you and me.

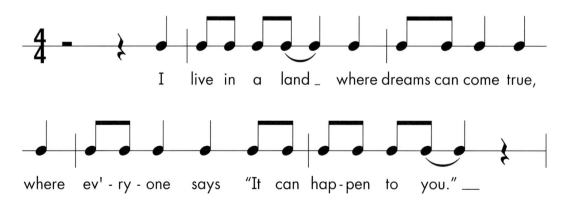

I live in a land _ where dreams can come true,

where ev'-ry-one says "It can hap-pen to you." _

Mar - tin had a dream that he could see, ___

And once up - on a time he was a kid like me. ___

Like me (like you), Like you (like me).

Mar - tin had a dream that he could see, ___

And once up - on a time he was a kid like me. ___

## Dreaming of Freedom

Martin Luther King, Jr. gave a famous speech called "I Have a Dream." He ended his speech with words from this spiritual.

**13-7**

# Free at Last

*African American Spiritual*

**REFRAIN**

Free at last, __ free at last, __

Thank God Al-might-y, I'm free at last, __

Free at last, __ free at last, __

Thank God Al-might-y, I'm free at last. __ *Fine*

**VERSE**

1. Way down yonder in the graveyard walk,
   Thank God Almighty, I'm free at last.
   Me and my Jesus gonna meet and talk,
   Thank God Almighty, I'm free at last. *Refrain*

2. On a my knees when the light passed by, . . .
   Thought my soul would rise and fly, . . . *Refrain*

3. Some of these mornings, bright and fair, . . .
   Gonna meet King Jesus in the air, . . . *Refrain*

# A Dream of Your Own

**Create** a call-and-response rap about your dreams. This poem might give you some ideas.

## When I Grow Up

*by Jack Prelutsky*

When I grow up, I think that I
may pilot rockets through the sky,
grow orchards full of apple trees,
or find a way to cure disease.
Perhaps I'll run for president,
design a robot, or invent
unique computerized machines
or miniature submarines.

When I grow up, I'd like to be
the captain of a ship at sea,
an architect, a clown or cook,
the writer of a famous book.
I just might be the one to teach
a chimpanzee the art of speech . . .
but what I'll *really* be, I'll bet
I've not begun to think of yet.

# Valentine's Day!

On Valentine's Day people show that they care about their friends and families. They give cards and gifts to one another.

In this Valentine song, you can **sing** about some unusual gifts. What is the form of the song?

13–8

# Valentines

*Words and Music by Burt Szabo*

**VERSE**

1. Don't you send me hearts and flow-ers   if you want to be   my
2. Don't you send me frogs and spi-ders   if you want to be   my

val - en - tine,   Send   me   frogs   and   hair-y-leg-ged spi-ders
val - en - tine,   Send   me   hearts and   choc-o-late __ flow-ers

if   you   want   to   be   my   val - en - tine.
if   you   want   to   be   my   val - en - tine.

Send me slugs and bugs and toads, cat - er - pil - lars, ants and
Send me cards with kitty cat smiles, but - ter - fly __ wings and

croc - o - diles, Send me snakes and a worm that squirms,
cud - dly bears, Send me straw - ber - ry tarts and cakes,

and then I'll be your val - en - tine.
and then I'll be your val - en - tine.

**REFRAIN**
*Chorus*

Bugs and but - ter -flies live to - geth - er, snakes and frogs and

kit - ty cats, too; All of us can live to - geth - er;

We can all be val - en - tines.

# Celebrate SPRING

People in many parts of the world celebrate the arrival of spring. In this folk song from Switzerland, part of the melody sounds like a bird. **Sing** the song, then name the bird.

13–10

## L'inverno è passato
### (Winter Is Over)

*English Words by Edith Bicknell*          *Folk Song from Switzerland*

L'in - ver - no  è  pas - sa - to,  l'a - pri - le  non c'è più,
The win - ter now is  o  - ver, and Ap - ril rains are gone;

è  rit - or - na - to il mag - gio  al  can - to  del  cu - cù.
It's May a - gain I know  for  I  hear the cuck-oo's song.

Cu - cù,        cu - cù,        l'a - pri - le  non  c'è  più;
Cuck - oo,      cuck - oo,      the  Ap - ril  rains  are  gone;

è  rit - or - na - to il mag - gio  al  can - to  del  cu - cù.
It's May a - gain I know  for  I  hear the cuck-oo's song.

# Springtime in Japan

In Japan the winters can be very cold. Japanese children sing this song to celebrate the arrival of spring. Move to show the direction of the melody.

## Haru ga kita
### (Springtime Has Come)

Japanese Words by Takano Tatsuyuki
English Words by Patty Zeitlin

School Song from Japan
Music by Okano Teiichi

1. Ha - ru ga ki - ta, ha - ru ga ki - ta
1. Spring - time has come, oh, spring - time has come, oh,

Do - ko ___ ni ki - ta? ___
How do you know it's true? ___

Ya - ma ni ki - ta, Sa - to ni ki - ta,
Look on the moun - tain, Down in the val - ley,

No ni - mo ki - ta. ___
In the prai - rie, too. ___

2. Hana ga saku, hana ga saku,
Doko ni saku?
Yama ni saku, Sato ni saku,
No nimo saku.

2. Flowers are blooming, Flowers are blooming,
Where are they in bloom?
Up on the mountain, Down in the valley,
In the prairie, too.

3. Tori ga naku, tori ga naku,
Doko de naku,
Yama de naku, Sato de naku,
No demo naku.

3. Birds are a-singing, Birds are a-singing,
Where can we hear them sing?
Up on the mountain, Down in the valley,
In the prairie, too.

# Celebrate America!

Patriotic songs tell about our country and our freedom. People of all ages sing patriotic songs to show pride in America.

**Sing** this song. Use dynamics to express the mood of the song.

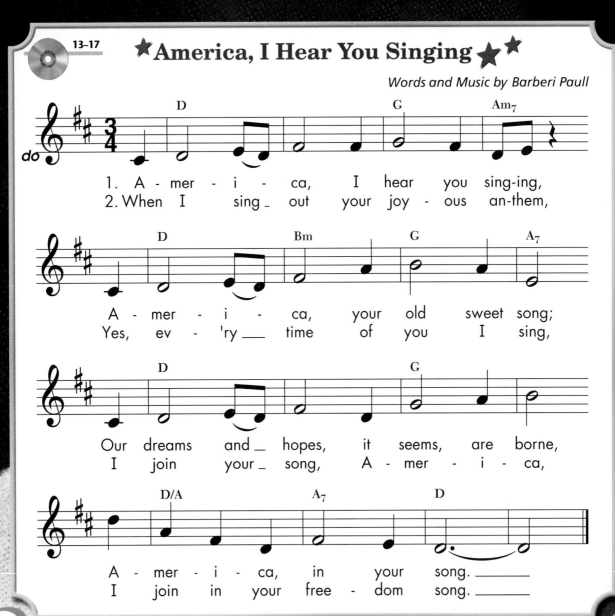

13–17

## ★America, I Hear You Singing ★★

*Words and Music by Barberi Paull*

1. A - mer - i - ca,  I  hear  you  sing-ing,
2. When  I  sing  out  your  joy - ous  an-them,

A - mer - i - ca,  your  old  sweet  song;
Yes,  ev - 'ry __ time  of  you  I  sing,

Our  dreams  and __ hopes,  it  seems,  are  borne,
I  join  your __ song,  A - mer - i - ca,

A - mer - i - ca,  in  your  song. ____
I  join  in  your  free - dom  song. ____

# America Sings!

Singing patriotic songs helps us to understand the people and the history of the United States.

**Sing** this famous patriotic song about the beauty of our land.

 13–19

 America

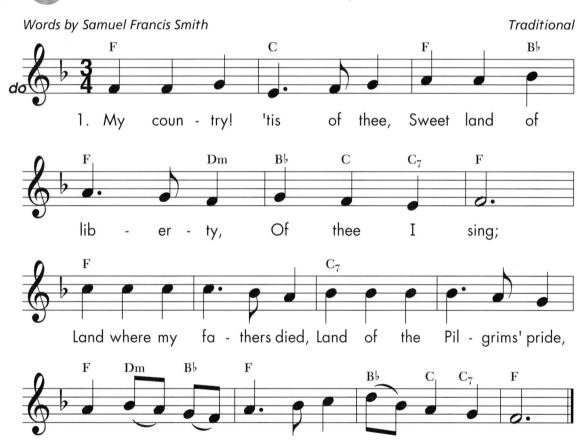

*Words by Samuel Francis Smith*                                          *Traditional*

1. My coun-try! 'tis of thee, Sweet land of
lib - er - ty, Of thee I sing;
Land where my fa - thers died, Land of the Pil - grims' pride,
From ev - 'ry __ moun - tain-side Let __ free - dom ring!

2. My native country, thee,
Land of the noble free,
Thy name I love;
I love thy rocks and rills,
Thy woods and templed hills;
My heart with rapture thrills
Like that above.

3. Let music swell the breeze,
And ring from all the trees
Sweet Freedom's song;
Let mortal tongues awake,
Let all that breathe partake,
Let rocks their silence break,
The sound prolong.

## A Marching Song

"Yankee Doodle" has been sung in America for
more than 200 years! Soldiers in America's
Continental Army sang this song as they
marched. Now you can **sing** it, too.

# ★★ Yankee Doodle ★★★

Words by Dr. Richard Shuckburgh

*Traditional*

1. Fath'r and I went down to camp,

A - long with Cap - tain Good - in',

And there we saw the men and boys

As thick as hast - y pud - din'.

**REFRAIN**

Yan - kee Doo - dle, keep it up, Yan - kee Doo - dle dan - dy,

Mind the mu - sic and the step And with the girls be hand - y.

2. And there was Captain Washington
Upon a slappin' stallion,
A-giving orders to his men;
I guess there was a million. *Refrain*

# Mallet Instruments

▲ Soprano xylophone

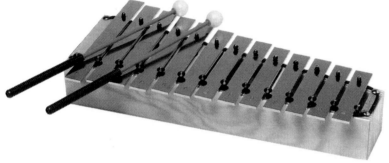

◀ Alto glockenspiel

## Holding the Mallets

It is important to hold the mallets correctly when you play mallet instruments.

▲

Hold the mallets in a relaxed way, almost as if you are riding a bike. Make sure you strike the bar in the center.

## Playing Borduns

You can play **borduns** on mallet instruments. Practice the borduns you see here.

**Borduns** are repeated patterns used to accompany music. They have two pitches, one of which is the home tone.

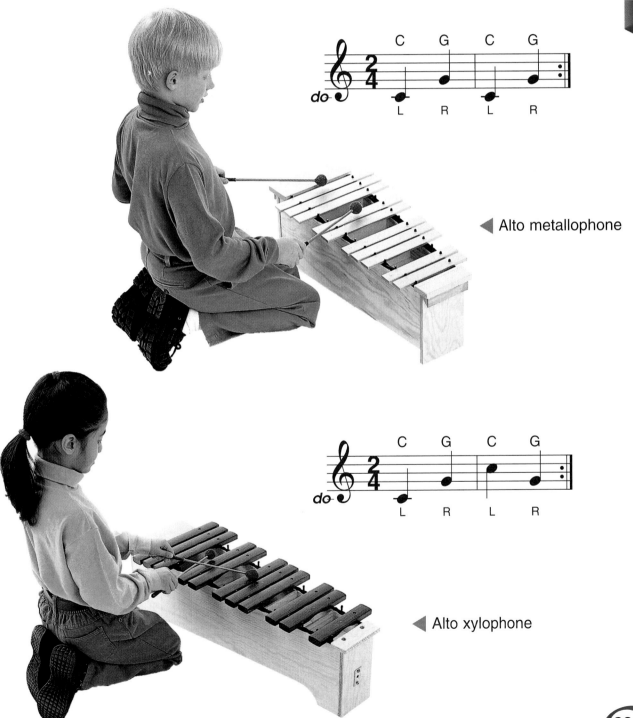

◀ Alto metallophone

◀ Alto xylophone

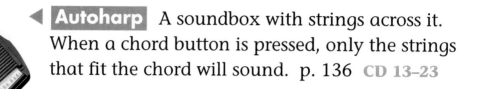

# Sound Bank

◀ **Autoharp** A soundbox with strings across it. When a chord button is pressed, only the strings that fit the chord will sound. p. 136 CD 13–23

◀ **Banjo** A string instrument similar to a guitar but smaller. It has metal strings and a round body. Banjos are often played in a style using fast picking or strumming. p. 119 CD 13–24

◀ **Cello** [CHEH-loh] A large wooden string instrument. The cello may be plucked with fingers or played with a bow. The cello has a rich, warm voice that can sound quite low. p. 136 CD 13–25

◀ **Clarinet** A wind instrument that has a mouthpiece with a reed. When the player blows into the mouthpiece, the air in the clarinet vibrates, making the sound. p. 174 CD 13–26

◀ **Conga** [KAHN-gah] An Afro-Cuban drum with a long barrel-shaped body. It comes in two sizes: the small quinto and the large tumbador. The conga is struck with the fingers and the palms of the hands. p. 214 CD 13–27

**Instrument Key:** strings percussion woodwind brass

**Cymbals** Curved metal plates that come in various sizes. Crash cymbals are played in pairs. The player holds one cymbal in each hand and quickly claps them together. Finger cymbals are tiny and make a delicate ringing sound. p. 6 CD 13–28

**Drum Set** A drum set, or kit, has several drums and cymbals including snare drum, bass drum, tom-toms, and cymbals. p. 67 CD 13–29

**Dulcimer (mountain)** An hourglass-shaped soundbox with three or four strings across it. The strings are usually plucked with a quill. The sound is quiet and sweet. p. 137 CD 13–30

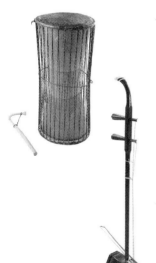

**Dundun** An African instrument with drum heads at each end joined by many strings. As the player strikes one drum head with a beater, the strings are pressed against the side and squeezed by the free arm to change the pitch. In that way the drum can imitate speech. p. 258 CD 13–31

**Erhu** [EHR-hoo] A Chinese string instrument played with a bow. It has only two metal strings. The tube has animal skin covering one end. p. 266 CD 13–32

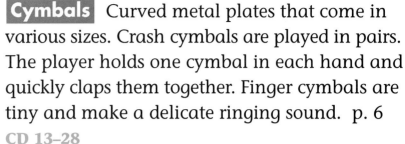

**Flute** A wind instrument shaped like a metal pipe. The player holds the flute sideways and blows across a mouthpiece. p. 6 CD 13–33

Sound Bank

Instruments in the Sound Bank usually appear on the pages listed. Some Sound Bank instruments are similar to other instruments in the lesson.

◀ **Guitar** A string instrument from Spain and Latin America, plucked with fingers or a pick. A guitar can play a melody. It can also play chords. Some guitars are electric. They can sound much louder. p. 137 CD 13–34

◀ **Hammered Dulcimer** A zither-type string instrument, also known as a cymbalom. Metal strings are stretched across bridges and played with spoon-shaped hammers. p. 136 CD 13–35

◀ **Koto** [KOH-toh] A Japanese string instrument with thirteen long strings. These are set high above the body of the instrument, which sits flat on the floor. The sound is a little like that of a harp. p. 136 CD 13–36

◀ **Maracas** Large round rattles with handles. They developed in the Caribbean area and in Venezuela. Shaking the maracas makes a crisp "swishing" sound. p. 171 CD 13–37

◀ **Marimba** A large barred instrument. The bars are made of rosewood and are struck with yarn mallets. Below the bars are resonating tubes that help carry the sound. p. 101 CD 13–38

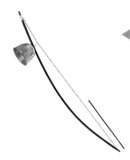

◀ **Musical Bow** A string instrument found in Africa. There are many kinds, but the one shown here has a bell attached to make the sound louder. This instrument sounds somewhat like large drops of water. p. 136 CD 13–39

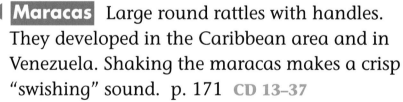

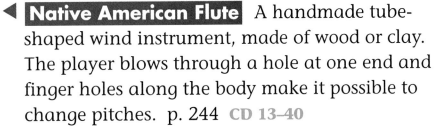

**Native American Flute** A handmade tube-shaped wind instrument, made of wood or clay. The player blows through a hole at one end and finger holes along the body make it possible to change pitches. p. 244 CD 13–40

*Pipa* [PEE-pah] A Chinese string instrument in the shape of a gourd. It has four strings and is one of the oldest of Chinese instruments. The pipa can play music in a quiet mood as well as in a loud "military style." p. 136 CD 13–41

*Shakuhachi* [shah-koo-HAH-chee] A Japanese wind instrument made of bamboo. The shakuhachi is a very well-known instrument in Japan. It is played with lots of pitch bends, clicks, and flutters. p. 324 CD 13–42

*Sheng* [shuhng] A Chinese mouth organ with a bowl-shaped wind chamber made of wood or metal. The sheng has 17 or 19 bamboo pipes of various sizes. The sound of the sheng can be shrill or pleasantly lyrical. p. 266 CD 13–43

**String Bass** A large wooden string instrument that is either plucked or bowed. The string bass is so tall that a player must stand up or sit on a high stool to play it. The voice of the string bass is deep, dark, and sometimes rumbling. p. 136 CD 13–34

Instruments in the Sound Bank usually appear on the pages listed. Some Sound Bank instruments are similar to other instruments in the lesson.

 **Synthesizer** An electronic instrument with a keyboard like a piano. It uses electricity in a special way to make sound. The synthesizer can make many sounds and imitate other instruments. p. 209 CD 13–45

 *Tabla* [TAH-blah] Hand drums from India. They are usually in sets of two or more. They have a variety of sounds—high, low, loud, pitched, unpitched—that can be produced by striking in different ways and on different parts of the drum head. p. 66 CD 13–46

 **Tambourine** A round instrument with small metal discs around the edge. Shaking or hitting the tambourine makes a jingling sound. p. 64 CD 13–47

**Timpani** Large bowl-shaped drums, also called kettledrums. Unlike many drums, timpani can be tuned to specific pitches. p. 66 CD 13–48

 **Trombone** A wind instrument made of brass. It makes sound the same way as the trumpet, but the pitches are lower. The player changes pitches by sliding a long curved tube up and down. p. 177 CD 13–49

**Trumpet** A wind instrument made of brass. It has a mouthpiece shaped like a little cup. The player makes the sound by "buzzing" the lips into the mouthpiece. The trumpet can sound very loud and military. p. 175 CD 13–50

◀ **Tuba** A very large brass instrument with a wide bell at one end of coiled tubing. The tuba's low notes are soft and dark-sounding. The higher ones are full and warm. p. 174 CD 13–51

◀ **Viola** [vee-OH-luh] A wooden string instrument that looks like a large violin. The viola is either bowed or plucked. The sound of the viola is deeper, richer, and darker than that of the violin. p. 137 CD 13–52

◀ **Violin** A string instrument that is usually played with a bow. It can also be plucked. The violin plays sounds from low to very high. p. 137 CD 13–53

◀ **Yangqin** [yahng-chin] A Chinese string instrument. It is placed flat on a stand and played with soft mallets. Each string has another underneath. When the string above is played, the one under it vibrates too, making a sweet sustained sound. p. 136 CD 13–54

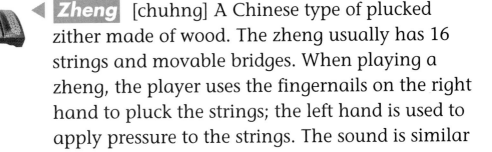

◀ **Zheng** [chuhng] A Chinese type of plucked zither made of wood. The zheng usually has 16 strings and movable bridges. When playing a zheng, the player uses the fingernails on the right hand to pluck the strings; the left hand is used to apply pressure to the strings. The sound is similar to a harp. p. 266 CD 13–55

**Sound Bank**

Instruments in the Sound Bank usually appear on the pages listed. Some Sound Bank instruments are similar to other instruments in the lesson.

# Glossary

**AB form** A musical plan that has two sections or parts. p. 165

**ABA form** A musical plan that has three sections or parts. The first and last sections are the same. The middle section is different. p. 197

**accent** Gives extra importance to a note in a rhythm pattern. p. 78

**accompaniment** Music that is performed to go with a melody. p. 140

**bar line** A vertical line drawn through a staff to separate measures. p. 83

**borduns** Repeated patterns used to accompany music. They have two pitches, one of which is the home tone. p. 391

**call and response** A style of choral singing. First one person sings the call and then the rest of the chorus sings a response, or an answer. p. 19

**coda** A short section added to the end of a song. p. 166

**crescendo** A word or music symbol that tells the performer to get gradually louder. p. 114

**cumulative song** A song that gets longer as each new verse is added. p. 346

**D.C. al Fine** An Italian phrase that tells the performer to go back to the beginning of the song and sing until the word *Fine*. p. 196

**dynamics** A word that describes the loudness or softness of music. p. 6

**fermata** A symbol that tells a performer to hold a note for an extra long time. p. 187

**form** The order of same and different ideas in music. p. 52

**improvise** To make up music as it is being performed. p. 215

**ledger line** An extra line used for pitches above or below the staff. p. 99

**legato** Describes a melody that has smooth, connected pitches p. 150

**measure** A grouping of beats separated by bar lines. p. 83

**melody** A row of pitches that move up or down or repeat. p. 25

**meter** The way beats of music are grouped together. They are often in sets of two or sets of three. p. 192

**note** A symbol for a musical sound. p. 78

**ostinato** A short repeated pattern. p. 35

**pentatonic** Songs that have only five pitches. p. 134

**percussion** Instruments that are played by shaking, scraping, or striking. p. 100

**phrase** A musical sentence. p. 124

**pitch** Another word for a musical note. Pitch is how high or how low a note sounds. p. 21

**pitch syllables** Syllables used to name pitches, for example: *do, re, mi, so,* and *la.* p. 27

**refrain** The section of a song that repeats, using the same melody and words. p. 187

**repeated pitches** Two or more pitches in a row that are the same. p. 61

**rhythm** A pattern of long and short sounds and silences. p. 10

**rhythm syllables** Syllables used to name specific rhythmic units. p. 17

**section** A part of a song or instrumental work. p. 164

**skip** Moving from one pitch to another, skipping one or more pitches in between. p. 61

**staccato** Describes a melody that has short, separated pitches. p. 150

**staff** A set of five horizontal lines on which music notes are written. p. 27

**steady beat** The regular pulse found in most music. p. 8

**step** Moving from one pitch to another with no skipped pitches in between. p. 61

**strong beat** The most important beat in a rhythm pattern. p. 50

**style** The special sound that is created when music elements, such as rhythm and timbre, are combined. p. 248

**technique** The special skill used to play an instrument. p. 65

**tempo** The speed of the beat in music. p. 42

**texture** How thin or thick the music sounds. p. 71

**tie** A musical symbol that joins two notes together to create a longer sound. p. 123

**timbre** The special sound each instrument makes. p. 64

Glossary

399

# Classified Index

## Folk, Traditional, and Regional Selections

# Holiday, Seasonal, and Special Occasion

# Listening Selections

## Poems and Stories

## Recorded Interviews

# Index of Songs

# and Speech Pieces

**Song Index**

# Credits

**Cover Photography:** Jade Albert for Scott Foresman
**Cover Design:** Steven Curtis Design, Inc.

## Photograph Credits

viii: Alain Espinosa viii: Jack Davis viii: Eileen Mueller Neill viii: Milan Kecman 1: H & E Bernheim/Woodfin Camp & Associates 2: © Bert Essel/The Stock Market 2: © Jim Erckson/The Stock Market 2: © Paul Barton/The Stock Market 3: (TL) © Mark Richards/PhotoDisc 3: PhotoDisc 4: © SpencerGrant/PhotoEdit 6: (CR) Robert Brenner/PhotoEdit 6: (BL) © Dean Berry/Liaison Agency 6: (CL) Tony Freeman/PhotoEdit 7: (R) Walt Disney Productions/Photofest 10: Joan Marcus (BC) ©Joan Marcus 10: Joan Marcus 11: Joan Marcus (TR) ©Joan Marcus 11: Joan Marcus (BR) ©Joan Marcus 28: (Bkgd) Artville 29: (TL) Collection of Mr. and Mrs. David C. Driskell 29: (Bkgd) Artville 30: (Bkgd) Artville 31: (Bkgd) Artville 43: (B) ©The Estate of Keith Haring 45: Dave G. Houser (TL) © Dave G. Houser 45: Dave G. Houser (B) © Dave G. Houser 47: (CR) Terry Vine/Stone 48: © Collections Mnam/Cci-Centre Georges Pompidou/"Photo: Phototheque des collections du Mnam/Cci" 48: (Bkgd) PhotoDisc 52: (Bkgd) PhotoDisc 53: (TR) Bernard Hoffman/Life Magazine, © Time Inc. 55: Ric Ergenbright (T) Ric Ergenbright/Ric Ergenbright 65: (BL) Brent Jones 66: Marilyn Rife (CL) Warren Johnson/Marilyn Rife 66: (CR) Jack Vartoogian 66: (B) Photograph by Michael Dames/Soh Daiko, New York 67: © Hulton-Deutsch Collection/Corbis 67: (Bk-Inside) Rudi Von Briel/PhotoEdit 67: (TL) ©Neil Zlozower/Neil Zlozower Photography 68: (BL) H & E Bernheim/Woodfin Camp & Associates 68: (BR) © Errington/The Hutchison Library 68: (T) The Newark Museum/Art Resource, NY 68: (T) PhotoDisc 69: (BR) Jack Vartoogian 69: (TL) © Mary Jelliffe/The Hutchison Library 69: (B) The Newark Museum/Art Resource, NY 73: (TR) Bernard Hoffman/Life Magazine, © Time Inc. 79: (TR) Nina Mera 79: (T) ©Estate of Roy Lichtenstein 82: (Bkgd) PhotoDisc 84: (Bkgd) Courtesy of WTTW, Chicago IL 84: (C) © Gianni Dagli Orti/Corbis 86: (Bkgd) Philip Gould/Corbis 88: (Bkgd) Philip Gould/Corbis 89: (R) Robert Fried Photography 91: (B) Photo © Jack Vartoogian 92: (BR) Glen Allison/Stone 92: (BL) Greg Probst/Stock Boston 93: (B) Black Star 93: (TR) Stephen Studd/Stone 96: (Bkgd) Corbis 101: (CR) Werner Forman/Art Resource, NY 102: (B) Tibor Bognar/Stock Market 102: (TR) Mark Lewis/Stone 103: Kuo-Huang Han Dr. Kuo-Huang Han 104: PhotoDisc 105: PhotoDisc 106: Michael Hays (Bkgd) Michael Hays 110: (C) Everett Collection, Inc. 110: Artville 112: Dave King/© Dorling Kindersley 112: © Dorling Kindersley 112: Flag Research Center 114: (Bkgd) Jon G. Fuller/Natural Selection Stock Photography, Inc. 116: (Bkgd) Jon G. Fuller/Natural Selection Stock Photography, Inc. 116: Jon G. Fuller/Natural Selection Stock Photography, Inc. 119: (BC) Gift of Mrs. Jane C. Carey as an addition to the Addie Burr Clark Memorial Collection, ©2000 Board of Trustees, National Gallery of Art, Washington, D.C. 139: Michael Le Poer Trench/Riverdance The Show 140: (B) Sitki Tarlan/Panoramic Images 140: (Bkgd) Planet Art 140: (B) Sitki Tarlan/Panoramic Images 141: (B) Sitki Tarlan/Panoramic Images 141: (B) Sitki Tarlan/Panoramic Images 143: (LR) Scala/Art Resource, NY 152: (TR) Pearl Corporation and Adams 152: (BL) Pearl Corporation and Adams 156: (Bkgd) PhotoDisc 172: (Bkgd) PhotoDisc 173: (Bkgd) PhotoDisc 175: (Bkgd) AP/Wide World 177: David Atlas (TL) ©David Atlas 178: (Bkgd) Michael Boys/Corbis 180: (C) PhotoDisc 185: (C) Frank Driggs Collection 198: © Charles Webb/©AppaLight 198: PhotoDisc 199: Kathleen Cunningham Private Collection Kathleen Cunningham 208: Big Briar 208: FotoSets 208: Big Briar 212: (Bkgd) Corbis 214: (Bkgd) © Staffan Widstrand/Corbis 218: Bill Bachmann/PhotoEdit 218: © Henry Diltz/Corbis 219: Joe Sohm/©Visions of America, LLC 2000 220: (CL) John Running/@2000 John Running 220: (TR) Teri Bloom Photography, Inc. 220: (B) © Kevin Fleming/Corbis 221: (BL) Daniel J. Gandor 221: (BR) © Joseph Sohm; ChromoSohm Inc./Corbis 221: (C) Photofest 222: (TC) © Joe Viesti/Viesti Collection, Inc. 222: (TL) SuperStock 223: © Jay Syverson/Corbis 234: (Bkgd) PhotoDisc 236: (Bkgd) Orion Press/Natural Selection Stock Photography, Inc. 236: (TR) PhotoDisc 237: (TL) SuperStock 237: (TR) Arthur Tilley/FPG International LLC 241: (TR) Artville 244: (Bkgd) Lynn Wozniak/All One Tribe, Inc. 245: (B) Peter B. Gallagher, Seminole Communications 246: (TR) AP/Wide World 248: (B) Fotos International/Archive Photos 249: (BL) Reed Saxon/AP/Wide World 256: (BR) Musee d'Orsay, Paris/Photograph by Erich Lessing/Art Resource, NY 256: (TR) Cary Wolinsky/Stock Boston 256: (TL) SuperStock 257: (TL) Bill Bachmann/PhotoEdit 258: (T) David Young-Wolff/PhotoEdit 259: (B) ©Victor Englebert 265: (B) © 1988/Brenda Joysmith Studio 268: (B) Photograph by Erich Lessing/Art Resource, NY 276: (TR) © H. Joseph Sohm/Visions of America 277: (CL) © Bob Torrez/Stone 277: (TR) © Robert Eckert/Stock Boston 277: Robert Amft (CL) Robert Amft 281: Banana Slug String Band 284: (Bkgd) © Mark Gamba/The Stock Market 284: (T) PhotoDisc 284: PhotoDisc 293: (TR) © Stephen Dalton/Photo Researchers, Inc. 296: (TR) Pictor 296: (Bkgd) © Algaze/Image Works 297: William Bollendorf (BL) Galerie Macondo 310: (L) Northwest Indian College 311: (BR) @2000 John Running 322: (B) Schalkwijk/Art Resource, NY 322: (Bkgd) SuperStock 326: (TR) Corbis 328: (Bkgd) © 1999 by Dan Andreasen/Courtesy, HarperCollins Publishers 329: (BR) © Henry Diltz/Corbis 332: PhotoDisc 333: PhotoDisc 334: (L) PhotoDisc 334: (L) PhotoDisc 334: PhotoDisc

Every effort has been made to obtain permission for all photographs found in this book and to make full acknowledgment for their use. Omissions brought to our attention will be corrected in subsequent editions.

**All other photos:** Pearson Learning and Scott Foresman

## Illustration Credits

1: Lyn Martin 1: Julie Peterson 1: Susan Spellman 2 - 4: Bert VanderMark 6: Rose Mary Berlin 8: Mary Ross 12 - 13: Georgia Cawley 14: Dom Lee 16: Alain Espinosa 18: Susan Swan 20 - 23: Joel Spector 24: Linda Graves 26: Franklin Hammond 32: Georgia Cawley 34: Jack Davis 37: Joel Spector 38 - 40: Bert VanderMark 44: Judy Jarrett 46: Terry Taylor 46: Kelly Hume 50: Guy Porfirio 51: Francesco Santalucia 54 - 55: Annette Cable 56 - 57: Winky Adam 58: Anthony Lewis 60 - 63: Jennifer Thermes 68: Mike Dammer 68: Kelly Hume 70: Donna Perrone 72: Jennifer Thermes 73: Donna Perrone 76: Michael Sternagle 76: Tom Foty 78: Georgia Cawley 80 - 81: Susan Spellman 81: Darryl Ligasan 82 - 83: Laura De Santis 86: Tim Huhn 90: Lorraine Ryan 94: Donna Perrone 98: Kandy Radsinski 100 - 101: David Diaz 104: George Hamblin 108: Susan Spellman 114: Kelly Hume 117: Tony Nuccio 118: Byron Gin 118: Kelly Hume 120: Sam Whitaker 122 - 123: Alexi Natchev 126: Fahimeh Amiri 128: Rusty Fletcher 130: Tim Spransy 130: Kelly Hume 132: Chi Chung 136: Francesco Santalucia 138: Kelly Hume 138: Tony Nuccio 142: Wendy Rasmussen 142: Kelly Hume 144: Rusty Fletcher 144: Francesco Santalucia 145: Chi Chung 146 - 149: Gwen Connelly 150: Lyn Martin 152: Linda Howard Bittner 152: Lyn Martin 153: Linda Howard Bittner 154: Marcela Cabrera 156 - 157: Chi Chung 158 - 161: Kathi Ember 162: Milan Kecman 164 - 166: Susan Swan 168 - 169: Mary Anne LLoyd 170: Higgins Bond 174: Fred Willingham 174: Marc Mongeau 175: Fred Willingham 176: Claude Martinot 178: Kelly Hume 181: Susan Swan 182 - 185: William Ersland 186 - 187: Diane Greenseid 188: Eileen Mueller Neill 190 - 193: Christopher Corr 196 - 197: Jared Lee 200 - 202: Milan Kecman 204: Julie Peterson 206: Tom Foty 209: Tony Nuccio 210: George Hamblin 216: Diane Greenseid 216: Tom Foty 216: Jared Lee 217: Milan Kecman 218: Higgins Bond 218: Joel Spector 218: Shelly Hehenberger 218: Jill Banashek 219: Eileen Mueller Neill 219: Jerry Tiritilli 219: Larry Reinhart 219: Higgins Bond 219, 224 - 227: C. D. Hullinger 230 - 233: Jerry Tiritilli 234: Beth Foster Wiggins 234: Kelly Hume 234: Beth Foster Wiggins 235: Joel Spector 236: Kelly Hume 238: Higgins Bond 240: Susan Swan 242: Joel Spector 244 - 245: Dorothy Sullivan 246: Pat Bailey 246: Kelly Hume 248: Pat Bailey 250 - 252: Ilene Robinette 260 - 261: Priscilla Burris 264: Jill Banashek 266: Cheryl Kirk Noll 268: Wayne McLoughlin 269: Tony Nuccio 270 - 271: Wayne McLoughlin 272: Brad Teare 274: Dorothy Sullivan 274 - 275: Kelly Hume 278 - 280: Gary Torrisi 282: Kristin Kest 286: Tom Foty 290: Donna Catanese 292: Jerry Tiritilli 294: Eileen Mueller Neill 298: Paul Larson 300 - 303: Larry Reinhart 304 - 307: Jill Banashek 308: Jane Dippold 310: Wayne Parmenter 312 - 314: Shelly Shinjo 318: Tim Huhn 324 - 326: Oki Han 327: Tony Nuccio 330: Higgins Bond 330: Kelly Hume 330: Susan Edison 336: Toby Williams 338 - 340: Peter Fasolino 342: Shelly Hehenberger 346: Georgia Cawley 348: Dan McGeehan 350: Teri Sloat 350: Kelly Hume 351: Matthew Wycislak 352: John Sandford 354 - 356: Dan McGeehan 359: Tony Nuccio 362 - 363: C. D. Hullinger 364: David Austin Clar 364: Kelly Hume 366: Gregg Thorkelson 368 - 369: Leslie Watkins 370 - 371: Karen Pritchett 372 - 374: Jeremy Tugeau 381: Higgins Bond 382: Nancy Tobin 316: Sam Whitaker

## Acknowledgments

Credit and appreciation are due publishers and copyright owners for use of the following: 4: "Gonna Have a Good Time" words and music by Bill Shontz, from *Rosenshontz: Share It!* 1992 Rosho Music. Reprinted by permission. 7: "Heigh-Ho" words by Larry Morey, music by Frank Churchill. © Copyright 1938 by Bourne Co. Copyright Renewed. This arrangement © 2001 by Bourne Co. All Rights Reserved. International Copyright Secured. 8: "Time to Sing" music by Raffi, words by Raffi, D. Pike, B & B Simpson. © 1985 Homeland Publishing (CAPAC). A division of Troubadour Records Ltd. All rights reserved. Used by permission. 12: "Go Around the Corn, Sally" from *Let's Get the Rhythm of the Band: A Child's Introduction to Music From African-American Culture With History and Song.* Words and music by Cheryl Warren Mattox. Copyright © 1993. Reprinted by permission. 16 "Un pajarito" (A Little Bird) ["El pájaro" (The Bird)] from *A Fiesta of Folk Songs from Spain & Latin America* by Henrietta Yurchenco, copyright © 1967 by Henrietta Yurchenco. Used by permission of G.P. Putnam's Sons, a division of Penguin Putnam Inc. English words © 2002 Pearson Education, Inc. 28: "Pizza, Pizza, Daddy-o" from *Circle 'Round the Zero* by Maureen Kenney and MMB Music, Inc. 1974. Reprinted by permission. 32: "Down, Down, Baby" © 2002 Pearson Education, Inc. 34: "Riddle Ree" words and rhythmic setting by Grace Nash from *Today With Music* by Grace Nash. © 1973 Alfred Publishing Co., Inc. Used with Permission of the Publisher. 40: "The Music's in Me" words and music by Jill Gallina. Copyright © 1985 by Jenson Publications. This arrangement copyright © 2001 by Jenson Publications. International Copyright Secured. All Rights Reserved. Used by permission. 44: "Gypsy in the Moonlight" (Folk Song from Trinidad), from *Caribbean Voyage: Brown Girl In The Ring.* Courtesy of the Alan Lomax Archives. 45: "Alligator Pie" words by Dennis Lee, from *Dinosaur Dinner (With a Slice of Alligator Pie)* by Jack Prelutsky. Text Copyright © 1974 by Dennis Lee. Reprinted by permission of Alfred A. Knopf Children's Books, a division of Random House, Inc. Also recorded by permission of the author from *Alligator Pie* (Macmillan of Canada, 1974). Rhythmic setting © 2002 Pearson Education, Inc. 50: "Way Down in the Schoolyard" from *In the*

*Schoolyard* by Sharon Lois & Bram. Used by permission of Elephant Records. 52: "Good Mornin', Blues" new words and new music arranged by Huddie Ledbetter. Edited and new additional material by Alan Lomax. TRO— © Copyright 1959 (Renewed) Folkways Music Publishers, Inc., New York, NY. Used by Permission. 54: "El juego chirimbolo" (The Chirimbolo Game) from *Roots and Branches: A Legacy of Multicultural Music for Children*, by Patricia Shehan Campbell, Ellen McCullough-Brabson, and Judith Cook Tucker. Courtesy World Music Press. English words © 2002 Pearson Education, Inc. 56: "Clouds of Gray" from *Kodaly in Kindergarten*, (BK-15) words and music by Katinka S. Daniel, copyright © 1981 Mark Foster Music Co., a Division of Shawnee Press, Inc. Delaware Water Gap, PA 18327. International Copyright Secured. All Rights Reserved. Reprinted by permission. 57: "Wind Has Shaken Autumn Down" by Tony Johnston. Copyright © 1990 by Tony Johnston. Reprinted by arrangement with Writers House LLC, as agent for the author. 58: "I See The Moon" words by Carl Withers, melody from *Let's Sing Together* by Denise Bacon. Copyright 1971 by Boosey & Hawkes, Inc. Copyright Renewed. Reprinted by permission of Boosey & Hawkes, Inc. 64: "Achshav" (Awake! Awake!) English words © 1995 Silver Burdett Ginn. 67: "De Beat" by Grace Nichols from *Treasury of Children's Poetry*. Reproduced with permission of Curtis Brown Ltd, London, on behalf of Grace Nichols. Copyright Grace Nichols 1989. 70: "Ayelivi" arranged by Komla Amoaku from the Ewe speaking people of Ghana. Reprinted by permission. English words © 2002 Pearson Education, Inc. 74: "Step In Time" words and music by Richard M. Sherman and Robert B. Sherman. © 1963 Wonderland Music Company, Inc. All Rights Reserved. Used by Permission. 78: "Boogie Chant and Dance" from *Rhythm Road: Poems to Dance To*. Words by Lillian Morrison. Copyright © 1988 by Lillian Morrison. Used by permission of HarperCollins Publishers. 79: "Two Little Sausages" from *Anna Banana: 101 Jump-Rope Rhymes* by Joanna Cole. Text copyright © 1989 by Joanna Cole. Used by permission of HarperCollins Publishers. Rhythmic setting © 2002 Pearson Education, Inc. 82: "Johnny Get Your Hair Cut." Reproduced by permission of the American Folklore Society from *American Folklore Memories* 39. Not for further reproduction. 83: "Jelly in a Dish" from *Anna Banana: 101 Jump-Rope Rhymes*. Words by Joanna Cole. Text copyright © 1989 By Joanna Cole. Used by permission of HarperCollins Publishers. Rhythmic setting © 2002 Pearson Education, Inc. 86: "Crawfish!" words and music by Papillion © 1997, Papillion Inc publisher. From the album *Cajun for Kids! Papillion*, Music for Little People/Label. Reprinted by permission. 90: "Ein Männlein steht im Walde" (A Little Man in the Woods), poem by Hoffmann von Fallersleben. Traditional music. Publication: *Sing Mit, Unterstufe*. Printed by R. Oldenbourg Verlag, München 1975. Used with permission. English words © 2002 Pearson Education, Inc. 92: "Allá en la fuente" (There at the Spring). From *Arroz Con Leche: Popular songs and Rhymes from Latin America*. Selected and illustrated by Lulu Delacre. Copyright © 1989 by Lulu Delacre. Reprinted by permission of Scholastic, Inc. English words © 2002 Pearson Education, Inc. 95: "Naranja dulce" (Sweet Orange) English words © 2002 Pearson Education, Inc. 96: "Rocky Mountain" folk song from Southern United States. © 1972 (Renewed) Belwin, Inc. All Rights Reserved. Used by Permission. WARNER BROS. PUBLICATIONS U.S. INC., Miami, FL 33014. 100: "Ise Oluwa" a Yoruba Song from Nigeria, arranged by Nitanju Bolande Casel. Copyright © 1989 by Nitanju Bolande Casel, Clear Ice Music. Used by permission. 105: "Waiting for the Traffic Light" © 2002 Pearson Education, Inc. 112: "Banana" from *Rainbow Sign*. Words and music by Flor de Caña. Reprinted by permission. 114: "La tormenta tropical" (The Tropical Storm) © 2000 Juanita Newland-Ulloa, ASCAP. 118: "Dinah" © 1995 Silver Burdett Ginn. 124: "A Song That's Just for You" © 2000 Bryan Louiselle and Frog Prince Music. 128: "Plant Four Seeds" from *Music For Children Volume 1*. American Version by Carl Orff and Gunild Keetman. © 1982 Schott Music Corp. All Rights Reserved. Used by Permission of European American Music Distributors LLC, Sole U.S. and Canadian Agent for Schott Music Corp. 130: "Mississippi River Chant" from *Sounds of a Powwow*, Words by Bill Martin Jr. Used with the permission of the author. 133: "Ha'kyo jung" (School Bell Sounding) words and music by Mary Kimm Joh from *Roots & Branches: A Legacy of Multicultural Music for Children* by Patricia Shehan Campbell, Ellen McCullough-Brabson, and Judith Cook Tucker. Courtesy World Music Press. English words © 2002 Pearson Education, Inc. 140: "Adana ya gidelim" (Let's Go to Adana) from *Sing Around the World* by Shirley W. McRae. English words © 2002 Pearson Education, Inc. 142: "Oh, Watch the Stars" from *Folk Songs North America Sings* by Richard Johnston. 1984 by Caveat Music Publishing Ltd., copyright assigned 1988 to G. Ricordi & Co. (Canada) Ltd. Used with permission. 146: "I See With My Hands" words and music by Marcy Marxer. From *Cathy and Marcy: Nobody Else Like Me*. © 1993 2 Spoons Music (ASCAP). Used with permission. 150: "Party Tonight!" © 2000 Jill Gallina. 154: "Mariposita" (Little Butterfly) words and music by Wilbur Alpírez Quesada, from *Los Niños Cantan: Canciones para kindergarden y escuela primaria* by Wilbur Alpírez Quesada, 1979. English words © 2002 Pearson Education, Inc. 156: "Hui jia qü" (Home from School) English words by David Eddleman. Reprinted by permission. 158: "Un elefante" (An Elephant) words and music by Claudina de Ferrari. English words © 2002 Pearson Education, Inc. 162: "Same Train" from *Sing a Song* by Charity Bailey © 1955 (renewed) Plymouth Music Co., Inc. Reprinted by permission. 164: "Clear the Kitchen" © 1988 Silver Burdett Ginn. 166: "Dinosaur Dance" words and music by Ned Ginsburg. © 1991 by Ned Ginsburg. Reprinted by permission. 168: "All Around the Buttercup," from *Let's Sing Together* by Denise Bacon. © Copyright 1971 by Boosey & Hawkes, Inc. Copyright renewed. Reprinted by permission of Boosey & Hawkes, Inc. 170: "Cookie" from *Leading Young Children to Music*, 6E by Haines and Gerber, © 2000. Reprinted by permission of Prentice-Hall, Inc., Upper Saddle River, NJ. 176: "Cheki, morena" (Shake It!) from *Roots and Branches: A Legacy of Multicultural Music for Children*, by Patricia Shehan Campbell, Ellen McCullough-Brabson, and Judith Cook Tucker. Courtesy World Music Press. English words © 2002 Pearson Education, Inc. 184: "The Flat Foot Floogee" words and music by Slim Gaillard, Bud Green, and Slam Stewart. © 1938 (Renewed) by Jewel Music Publishing Co., Inc. (ASCAP) in the United States. This arrangement Copyright © 2001 by Jewel Music Publishing Co., Inc. (ASCAP) Holliday Publications (ASCAP) and O Vouti Publishing (ASCAP) in the United States. All Rights for O Vouti Publishing Administered by Quartet Music, Inc. International Copyright Secured. All Rights Reserved. Used by permission. 186: "But the Cat Came Back" words and music by Josef Marais. (ASCAP) © 1956, 1984. Used by permission of Marcel Demiranda. 189: "Caballito blanco" (Little White Pony) from *Songs in Action* by R. Phyllis Gelineau, 1974. English words © 2002 Pearson Education, Inc. 191: "Boysie" from *The Melody Book* by Patricia Hackett. © 1983. Reprinted by permission of Prentice-Hall, Inc., Upper Saddle River, NJ. 193: "Sleep, Baby, Sleep" from *Shake It To The One That You Love Best* adapted by Cheryl Warren Mattox. Reprinted by permission. 197: "Flies" from *All Together* by Dorothy Aldis, copyright 1925-1928, 1934, 1939, 1952, renewed 1953, © 1954-1956, 1962 by Dorothy Aldis, © 1967 by Roy E. Porter, renewed. Used by permission of G.P. Putnam's Sons, a divison of Penguin Putnam Inc. 198: "Trouble Is a Mountain" words and music by Arthur Cunningham. 1979. Used by permission of Mrs. Arthur Cunningham. 204: "See-Saw Sacradown" music by Paul Kapp. 208: "Free Music No. 1" tracing of a score by Percy Grainger. Reproduced by kind permission of Bardic Edition. 211: "Rosie, Darling Rosie" © Copyright 1974 by Boosey & Hawkes, Inc. Reprinted by permission of Boosey & Hawkes, Inc. 212: "The Animals Find Water" © 1991 Silver Burdett Ginn. 222: "Ev'ry Kind of Music" words and music by David Eddleman. © 1991 David Eddleman. All rights reserved. 223: "Way Down in the Music" by Eloise Greenfield from *Honey I Love*. Text copyright © 1978 by Eloise Greenfield. Reprinted by permission of HarperCollins Publishers. 224: "Glad to Have a Friend Like You" from *Free to Be...You and Me*. Words and music by Carol Hall. © Copyright 1999 Otay Music, Corp. and Daniel Music (ASCAP). Reprinted by permission. 228: "Bob-a-Needle" © 2002 Pearson Education, Inc. 236: "We're All Gonna Shine Tonight" music and lyrics by Marie Winn and Allan Miller from the *Fireside Book of Fun and Games* published by Simon & Schuster. Music and lyrics copyright © 1966, renewed 1994 by Marie Winn and Allan Miller. Reprinted by permission. 238: "I Got Shoes" © 2002 Pearson Education, Inc. 242: "El florón" (The Flower) English words © 1995 Silver Burdett Ginn. 245: "Duck Dance" © 1998 Seventh Generation Music. 246: "Peppermint Twist" words and music by Joey Dee and Henry Glover. © 1961, 1962 (Copyrights Renewed) EMI Longitude Music Co. All Rights Reserved. Used by Permission. WARNER BROS. PUBLICATIONS U.S. INC., Miami, FL 33014. 250: "Around the World" © 2002 Pearson Education, Inc. 252: "All the Way Around the World" words and music by Katherine Dines. Copyright © Kiddie Korral Music. Reprinted by permission. 254: "Hello!" words and music by Laszlo Slomovits. © 1988 ASCAP. Used by permission. 257: "Sawatdee tuh jah" (The Hello Song) © 1998 Silver Burdett Ginn. 261: "Zudio" © 1995 Silver Burdett Ginn. 262: "Kapulu kane" (Puili Game Song) from *Leading Young Children to Music*, 6E by Haines/Gerber, © 2000. Reprinted by permission of Prentice-Hall, Inc. Upper Saddle River, NJ. 267: "Diou shou juan'er" (Hide the Scarf) a Game Song from China from *Roots and Branches: A Legacy of Multicultural Music for Children* by Patricia Shehan Campbell, Ellen McCullough-Brabson, and Judith Cook Tucker. Courtesy World Music Press. English words © 2002 Pearson Education, Inc. 270: "Mon papa" (My Papa) © 2002 Pearson Education, Inc. 272: "Somebody Waiting" © 2002 Pearson Education, Inc. 275: "Haere" (Farewell) traditional Maori Song, edited and arranged by Patricia Shehan Campbell, Sue Williamson, and Pierre Perron. © 1996 Warner Bros. Publications. All Rights Reserved. Used by permission. WARNER BROS. PUBLICATIONS U. S. INC., Miami, FL 33014. English words © 2002 Pearson Education, Inc. 276: "I'm Flying Home" words and music by David Eddleman. © 1991 David Eddleman. Used by permission. All rights reserved. 278: "What Do Animals Need?" by the Banana Slug String Band. Reprinted by permission. 282: "El coquí" (The Little Frog) from *De Colores and Other Latin Folk Songs for Children* by José-Luis Orozco, copyright © 1994 by José-Luis Orozco. Used by permission of Dutton Children's Books, a division of Penguin Putnam, Inc. and José-Luis Orozco. Recordings for this selection and others by José-Luis Orozco are available from Arcoiris Records, P.O. Box 7482, Berkeley CA 94707. 284: "Listen to the Water" words and music by Bob Schneider. © 1980 Bobally Music. All Rights Reserved. Reprinted by permission. 287: "Chawe chidyo chem'chero" a story-song from Zimbabwe, from *African Story-Songs: Told and Sung by Dumisani Maraire*. Copyright 1969, University of Washington Press, used by permission. 290: "Der sad to katte" (Two Cats) from *Musikbogen O*, by Erling Bisgaard and Gulle Stehower. Copyright © 1974 by Editions Wilhem Hansen AS, Copenhagen. International Copyright

Secured. All Rights Reserved. Reprinted by permission of G. Schirmer, Inc. (ASCAP) 294: "Rabbit Footprints" © 1991 David Eddleman. Used by permission. All rights reserved. 295: "Rabbits" by Noah Wager. Reprinted by permission of the author. 296: "Deau-deau, ti pitit maman" (Sleep, My Little One) © 2002 Pearson Education, Inc. 300: "Lots of Worms" words and music by Patty Zeitlin. Reprinted by permission of Folklore Productions (ASCAP). 306: "Don't Dump Trash" words and Music by Jill Jarboe. Copyright © 1999 Smithsonian Folkways Recordings. SF 45048 Coco Kallis: Environmental Songs for Kids. "Don't Dump Trash" provided courtesy of Smithsonian Folkways Recordings (202) 287-3424. Reprinted by permission. 307: "Breaks Free" from Cactus Poems, poems by Frank Asch. Text copyright ©1998 by Frank Asch. Reprinted by permission of Harcourt, Inc. 308: "Every Morning When I Wake Up" words and music by Avon Gillespie. © 1976 Belwin-Mills Publishing Corp. All Rights Reserved. Used by Permission. WARNER BROS. PUBLICATIONS U. S. INC., Miami, FL 33014. 310: "Tall Cedar Tree" © 1999 Pauline Hillaire. 311: "The Rain Song" from Yazzie Girl by Sharon Burch. Copyright © 1989 by Sharon Burch. Reprinted by permission of Canyon Records. 312: "Who Has Seen the Wind?" from Sing for Joy edited and compiled by Norman and Margaret Mealy. © 1961 by The Seabury Press, Inc. 314: "To a Red Kite" from I Thought I Heard the City by Lilian Moore. Copyright © 1969 Lilian Moore. © Renewed 1997 Lilian Moore. Used by permission of Marian Reiner for the author. 315: "Let's Go Fly a Kite" words and music by Richard M. Sherman and Robert B. Sherman. © 1963 Wonderland Music Company, Inc. All Rights Reserved. Reprinted by permission. 316: "Falling Rain" music by April K. Kassirer, words by Susan Marcus, from the recording Homefree! (© SOCAN) Used by permission. 318: "Zip-a-Dee-Doo-Dah" words by Ray Gilbert, music by Allie Wrubel. Copyright © 1945 Walt Disney Music Company. All Rights Reserved. Used by permission. 320: "The Rainbow" by Jean R. Thomas, from Songs for Very Little Folks, © 1981 Jean R. Thomas. Used with permission. 323: "En nuestra Tierra tan linda" (On Our Beautiful Planet Earth) from Diez Deditos by José-Luis Orozco, copyright © 1997 by José-Luis Orozco, text and musical arrangements. Used by permisson of Dutton Children's Books, a division of Penguin Putnam Inc. and José-Luis Orozco. Recordings for this selection and others by José-Luis Orozco are available from Arcoiris Records, P.O. Box 7482, Berkeley CA 94707. 324: "Tanabata-sama" (Star Festival) Japanese words by Hanayo Gondo and Ryuha Hayashi. Music by Kan-ichi Shimofusa. Copyright © 1960 by Edward B. Marks Music Company. This arrangement copyright © 2001 by Edward B. Marks Music Company. Copyright Renewed. International Copyright Secured. All Rights Reserved. Used by Permission. English words © 1998 Silver Burdett Ginn. 330: "From Sea to Shining Sea" words and music by Gene Grier and Lowell Everson. © 1991 Heritage Music Press, a division of the Lorenz Corporation International copyright secured. All rights reserved. Used by permission. 332: "Sing Me a Story" © 2000 Jill Gallina. 336: "Puff, the Magic Dragon" words and music by Peter Yarrow and Leonard Lipton. © 1963 Pepamar Music Corp. © Renewed, assigned to Silver Dawn Music and Honalee Melodies. All Rights Reserved. Used by Permission. WARNER BROS. PUBLICATIONS U.S. INC., Miami, FL 33014. 340: "Kibungo" from The Singing Sack: 28 Song-Stories from Around the World, compiled by Helen East, A & C Black (Publishers) Limited, 1989. Reprinted by permission of the publisher. English words © 2002 Pearson Education, Inc. 341: "O pião entrou" (The Top Joined the Circle) from The Singing Sack: 28 Song-Stories from Around the World, compiled by Helen East, A & C Black (Publishers) Limited, 1989. Reprinted by permission of the publisher. English words © 2002 Pearson Education, Inc. 343: "The Stars Streaming in the Sky" from "Wintu: The North Star" by William Brandon from The Magic World, 1991. Reprinted with the permission of Ohio University Press, Athens, Ohio. 348: "The Crocodile" © 1995 Silver Burdett Ginn. 350: "Deux Cocodries" (Two Crocodiles) used by permission from Le Hoogie Boogie: Louisiana French Music for Children by Sharon Arms Doucet. English words © 2002 Pearson Education, Inc. 352: "Jig Along Home" words and music by Woody Guthrie. TRO— © Copyright 1951 (Renewed) 1963 (Renewed) Ludlow Music, Inc., New York NY. Used by Permission. 356: "Look Out Below!" © 2000 Bryan Louiselle and Frog Prince Music. 358: "It's a Celebration!" © 2000 Katherine Dines. 360: "Vamos a la fiesta" (Let's Go to the Party) words and music by Juanita Newland-Ulloa from Canta Conmigo (Sing With Me), Bilingual Audio and Songbook Series Vol. 1-3 by Juanita Newland-Ulloa, www.juanitamusic.com. Reprinted by permission. 362: "Skin and Bones" based on a Kentucky folk song, collected and edited (new and additional words and music) by Jean Ritchie © 1952 Jean Ritchie Geordie Music Publishing Co. Reprinted by permission. 363: "The Owl and the Pumpkin" from Halloween on Parade (GF-72). Words by Betty Barlow and Victoria Shima, music by Betty Barlow. Copyright © 1977 Shawnee Press, Inc. Delaware Water Gap, PA 18327. International Copyright Secured. All Rights Reserved. Reprinted by permission. 364: "Perot" (Fruit) a folksong which appeared in Songs of Childhood selected and edited by Judith Eisenstein and Frieda Prensky, published 1955 by the United Synagogue Commission on Jewish Education. Used with permission. English words © 2002 Pearson Education, Inc. 366: "Thanksgiving Is Near" by Grace Nash. © 1988 Alfred Publishing Co., Inc. Used with per-

mission of the publisher. 367: "Setting the Thanksgiving Table" copyright 1991 by X.J. Kennedy. Published in The Kite That Braved Old Orchard Beach; published by Margaret K. McElderry Books, a division of Simon & Schuster Books for Young Readers. Reprinted by permission of Curtis Brown, Ltd. 368: "Chanukah Is Here!" a song which appeared in Songs of Childhood selected and edited by Judith Eisenstein and Frieda Prensky, published 1995 by the United Synagogue Commission on Jewish Education. Words for this song by Judith Eisenstein, music by Frieda Prensky. Used by permission. 369: "Ner Li" (The Light) words by Levin Kipnis and music by Mifalei Tarbuth Vekhinukh, Acum, Israel. Lyrics by the author, Acum, Israel. Used by permission of Acum Ltd. English words © 1995 Silver Burdett Ginn. 370: "O laufet, ihr Hirten" (Come Running, You Shepherds) from The International Book of Christmas Carols by Ehret/Evans, © 1964. Reprinted by permission of Prentice-Hall, Inc., Upper Saddle River, NJ. 371: "It's Santa—Again!" from Come Join In! 52 New Rounds, Partner Songs and Short Songs. Words and music by Elizabeth Gilpatrick. © 1996 Alfred Publishing Co., Inc. Used with permission of the publisher. 375: "Mister Snow Rap" © 2002 Pearson Education, Inc. 376: "A Kwanzaa Carol" © 1999 Reijiro Music. 378: "A Kid Like Me" words and music by Cathy Fink and Marcy Marxer, from Nobody Else Like Me, by Cathy Fink and Marcy Marxer. © 1993, 2 Spoons Music (ASCAP). Rounder Kids CD 8021. Used with permission. 380: "Free at Last" © 1995 Silver Burdett Ginn. 381: "When I Grow Up" by Jack Prelutsky, from A Pizza the Size of the Sun. Text copyright © 1996 by Jack Prelutsky. Used by permission of HarperCollins Publishers. 382: "Valentines" by Burt Szabo. Copyright 1999 by Choral Concepts. Reprinted by permission of Burt Szabo. 384: "L'inverno è passato" (Winter Is Over) © 2002 Pearson Education, Inc. 385: "Haru ga kita" (Springtime Has Come) words and music by Okano Teiichi and Patty Zeitlin. Reprinted by permission of Folklore Productions. 386: "America, I Hear You Singing" words and music by Barberi Paull. © 1991 by Barberi Paull. Reprinted by permission.

The editors of Scott Foresman have made every attempt to verify the source of "Kou ri lengay" (The Strength of the Lion) (p. 213), and "Ciranda" (A Ring of Roses) (p. 264), but were unable to do so. We believe them to be in the public domain. Every effort has been made to locate all copyright holders of material used in this book. If any errors or omissions have occurred, corrections will be made.

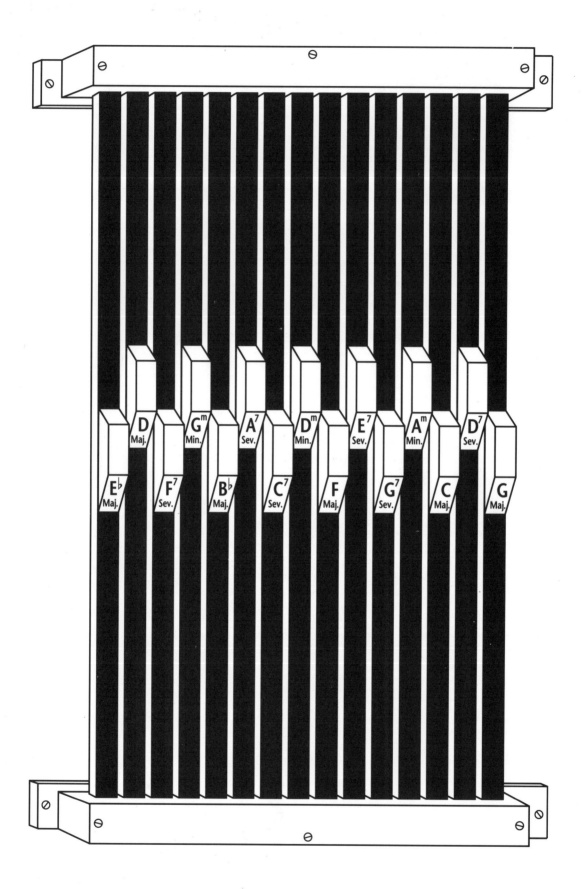